Becoming a Human Engineer

A Philosophical Inquiry into Engineering Education as Means or Ends

By

Alan Cheville

Becoming a Human Engineer: A Philosophical Inquiry into Engineering Education as Means or Ends

By Alan Cheville

This book first published 2022

Ethics International Press Ltd, UK

British Library Cataloguing in Publication Data

A catalogue record for this book is available from the British Library

Print Book ISBN: 978-1-871891-75-1

eBook ISBN: 978-1-871891-76-8

Contents

PREFACE & PROBLEM

Between the idea
And the reality
Between the motion
And the act
Falls the Shadow

- T.S. Eliot, "The Hollow Men"

There are many reasons to attempt writing a book. Probably the best is that over time stories, ideas, and questions build up inside that have to be shared, and a book is still the best way to organize thoughts you wish to share with others. Among the worst reasons if you happen to be an academic is that you have to write in order to get promoted or otherwise justify your existence. I am privileged that my reasons for writing align more with the former but as an academic there is always the niggling feeling in the back of my mind I are not doing quite enough or my work somehow lacks relevance. It is worth naming this feeling since it has a strong effect on our well-being as persons; that feeling is fear. Fear and love are major sub-themes of this book, and I hope to explore with the help of philosophy what fear and love mean in the context of engineering education. As an academic I identify my field as engineering education, a field I came to, like many of my generation, indirectly. In my case it was through more traditional research in electrical engineering. What brought me to engineering education were frustrations with teaching which caused me to reflect on lapses in my own education. What kept me in engineering education were the friends and community I found there. Friendship and community are other themes of this book.

In this book I seek to explore my increasing internal doubts about being an engineering educator. At a pragmatic level these doubts seem strangely misplaced since by objective measures these are good times for engineering education. National interest in STEM education is waxing due to its perceived influence on the economy and interest from policy makers often results in access to resources. The growing interest in engineering education has led to PhD programs being established at some universities and growing respect for the field, discipline, or whatever you wish to call it. Graduates of these programs are finding jobs, and universities are increasingly focusing on the importance of student learning. While engineering education at many universities still lacks the status of more established engineering disciplines, it is addressing challenging and important problems. The challenge for engineering education is that it works with humans who are naturally inhomogeneous, and its importance is that the diversity that plays havoc with data enables dynamic and free societies to exist. In engineering education people matter; technological problems are at their root human problems, and always have moral and ethical aspects. Engineering education is relevant because we are preparing those who will create our increasingly human-built world and our work indirectly affects the lives of billions of people.

Despite these positive aspects as my attention began to shift in scale, from the classroom and curriculum to national and societal issues, I began to doubt if my work as an engineering educator really served a larger good. My doubts are not about the importance or effectiveness of work in engineering education, they are not that meaningful change isn't happening, the doubts are whether what we are doing is morally defensible. There are numerous reasons to try to lay these doubts to rest, to ignore the nagging feeling that something isn't quite right. All the well-rehearsed arguments for the societal benefits of engineering and why we should invest in educating engineers are valid. Engineering offers rewarding careers, grows the economy, supports business, improves lifestyles, and often helps societies recover from crises. As we co-create an increasingly human-built world in which technology is necessary to maintain not only lifestyles but life itself, all of us come to rely more and more on the mostly invisible labor of engineers. The vision for engineering first stated by Tredgold in 1828 still guides engineers today: *"…being the art of directing the great sources of power in Nature for the use and convenience of man…"* These very real accomplishments have been achieved because for over a century engineering has been the willing partner of business and government, the practical production side of real-world industrialization, defense, and capitalism. This relationship has brought great benefits to many as evidenced by the unprecedented rise of standards of living in industrialized countries over the last century, continuing advances against persistent social ills, and historically unparalleled progress. It has also provided purpose to engineering which seeks to advance technology, increase production, reduce cost, and utilize natural forces for human good.

Yet despite these unquestioned successes the economic benefit of engineering seems increasingly disconnected from its personal meaning. I believe students are increasingly recognizing that engineering has become the path to a comfortable life, but perhaps not necessarily the path to a good one. My quiet crisis about engineering education is not one of too few engineers, students unprepared for the profession, or our inability to change the education system, but rather one of meaning, of purpose. The questions of purpose arise from the fact that the same factors that have led engineering to be successful are also contributing to negative systemic side effects—on environment, climate, and societal equity—that can no longer be conveniently ignored. The dilemma I perceive is that continuing on our current course leads to success in the short term and potential catastrophe in the long term. Again, the data cannot be ignored. The planet is warming at a potentially catastrophic rate due to the over-use of fossil fuels, technology-fueled neoliberal capitalism has led to increasing economic inequities, we have entered an Anthropocene age that is wreaking havoc on the other species that co-inhabit our environment, and information technology has prioritized profit and convenience over community leading to societal unraveling. We are also in a time in which groups around the world that have suffered various forms of oppression or injustice are seeking to be recognized and to participate fully in civic affairs. To create a more just society it will be necessary to increase participation of these groups in governance processes at all levels. Injustice and catastrophe seem tightly coupled. Addressing systemic issues will require collaboration across national boundaries, ethnic and religious identities, and the ability to bring all voices to the table, each of whom must be given trust and respect. If engineering cannot bring itself to reflect this diversity it will not have the moral authority it needs to address systemic challenges. If the lack of representation in engineering degree programs in the US represents a societal injustice, then what are the moral consequences of seeking to improve engineering education without first addressing equal representation?

There are some who will say these aren't the fault of engineering or the education that prepares engineers, rather it is larger issues in society and how others use, or perhaps misuse, technology that lead to negative outcomes. These arguments seem specious for several reasons. First, they assume there are limited and assignable causes and effects for systemic, societal problems. Not only are there not, but blaming others is ultimately futile; we must first look to our own role in the issues we create. Second, if as engineering educators we hold some responsibility for the world's problems then it seems unlikely that we can educate or engineer our way out of the problems we have created. These questions and tensions for engineering aren't going to be addressed by engineering a solution or through another blue-ribbon panel report addressing pragmatic questions with a generous side helping of self-promotion. Confronting whether educating engineers constitutes acting for moral good requires asking more existential and metaphysical questions; questions that are internal, reflective, and deeply philosophical.

Another way of framing my doubts about the good I am accomplishing as an engineering educator is to frame a dilemma I believe is faced by engineering education. A dilemma is different than the rhetorical device of crisis used in many policy reports. In a dilemma there is a forking of possibilities with no clear choice that one option will be better than the other. A dilemma is not a crisis, it demands a decision, not a solution, and often a difficult one. From my perspective one choice leads to teaching engineering as an increasingly esoteric discipline that dives deeper and deeper into rapidly branching pathways of technology where we must focus on objective truths to drive increasingly sophisticated technologies. The other choice involves recognizing we increasingly live in a built social world and technology has become an integral part of our inter-subjective and inter-objective reality. The first path leads to a highly scientific and technical discipline developing increasingly sophisticated technologies that drive economic growth and give some humans greatly increased capabilities and wealth. In my own view falling down this rabbit-hole leads eventually to a Carolingian world in which miracles are common, but it becomes increasingly difficult to make sense of reality and in which inequities abound. The second pathway recognizes that in a constructed world engineering is as connected to the social sciences and the humanities as much as it is to the physical sciences. Here we face difficult choices in how technology affects both the objective reality we depend on for our survival and the inter-subjective reality we have constructed and through which we increasingly create meaning for ourselves. Technology replicates, concentrates, and rapidly distributes ideas or paradigms. It forms a crucible through which we can develop a worldview that affects both our perceptions and actions. Engineering educators will have a vital role in determining which of these pathways we will follow.

This book is an attempt to explore these doubts, try to answer some of the questions that more traditional research can't, and from these explorations develop some small part of a philosophy of engineering education. As will be discussed later, philosophy matters since while research can help us find the right way to do something, it provides little guidance on what is right to do. The 20th century Scottish philosopher John Macmurray, whose work serves as the basis for this book, thought that practical philosophy was needed when old reasons for being no longer sufficed to keep a culture vital. Macmurray termed this vital force "faith", and when faith wanes disillusionment sets in and life loses its meaning. I start this journey with the view that much of what we have inherited from a century of rich tradition in engineering no longer fits us. Or as the Ent Treebeard says to Galadriel in J.R.R. Tolkien's *The Lord of the Rings* [1]: *"For the world is changing: I feel it in the water, I feel it in the earth, and I smell it in the air."*   It is time to reexamine the ends towards which engineering education was proposed as a means at the start of the 20th century. The challenge of engineering is no longer to tame science for industrial use, but rather to tame industry for humanity and the planet. This is not a book about what engineering education is, it is about what engineering education might become.

There are many I must thank who have had a role, direct or indirect, in the writing of a book. I must give sincere thanks to John Heywood who started me on this path through a chance conversation at the Frontiers in Education conference in Saratoga Springs back in 2008. Your mentorship and guidance over many years of Skype calls has been invaluable to my own continuing development. Thanks are also owed to Donna Riley and Linda Vanasupa who embody what it means to be courageous as an engineering educator. I also owe thanks to two mentors. From Sue Kemnitzer I learned that in an organization doing less often means accomplishing more and from Roger Burton the ability to set aside old ways of thinking. There are many within the engineering education community whose work over the long term have served to actually make it a community. These include Karl Smith and Cindy Atman; let us hope we never lose that value. I would also like to thank my colleagues at Bucknell who have patiently put up with the practical consequences of having a department chair interested in philosophy. I also must acknowledge material support from the National Science Foundation under Grant No. EEC-2022271 with the proviso that ny opinions, findings, and conclusions or recommendations expressed in this material are those of the author(s) and do not necessarily reflect the views of the National Science Foundation. And last but very much not least is my wife Karen who when we were both younger put up with my naïve and hubris-filled observations that the social sciences were not real science.

1
INTRODUCTION & CONTEXT

"Our freedom realizes itself in and through friendship."

Macmurray, *Freedom in The Modern World*, p. 117

Engineering education is in either a renaissance or crisis; likely both simultaneously with the difference depending one's point of view. While it sets a high bar, it may be fair to say that higher education, of which engineering education is a part, may be at the dawn of a paradigm shift. The term "paradigm shift" comes from Thomas Kuhn's *The Structure of Scientific Revolutions* [2] and in the context of science it means that ways of thinking are changing in response to new evidence. The term paradigm dates to the 15th Century and is derived from the Greek words for show and compare. So a paradigm is to compare options side by side which implies making a choice of one over the other. In Kuhn's use a paradigm shift occurs when new evidence is strong enough to force a choice in ways of thinking towards adopting new modes. If a nascent paradigm shift in engineering education is occurring a small part is due to new scientific evidence of how students learn, but the larger part arises from external forces that are raising questions about the value of a college degree and how education should serve society. Such questions do not constitute a Kuhnian paradigm shift based on scientific evidence that points the way to better understanding, rather they frame tensions [3] that raise new questions.

The sources of these tensions are economic, societal, and technological. At the time this book was written it seems that a college degree has never been more necessary or less affordable. Data is clear that college is one of the best investments an individual can make to their economic success [4]. Also the ways of knowing, acting, and being [5] developed in college STEM programs are in demand in an increasing number of jobs [6]. Yet in the United States the cost of college has been rising for nearly two decades at a higher rate than inflation [7]. Other countries have different funding models of higher education but many face similar affordability crises. Combined with high and increasing levels of income inequality [8] college is becoming outside of the reach of more and more people unless they are willing to take out significant loans. Rising indebtedness, however, is seen to create its own economic issues [9]. For these and other more political reasons universities have become media punching bags. Stories of disengaged students, pampered faculty, and country club environments abound. Yet the lived experiences of most students and faculty do not align with these caricatures. Most of those in the higher education system — students, faculty, staff, and administrators — are well intentioned, hard-working, and very devoted to their work. The hours are long, the pay just OK given their qualifications, and for many the choice to work in education is a form of service as well as a job. Yet the data does not lie. Costs are rising, debt increasing, and the difficult financial exigencies of most traditional universities provide no easy solution to containing the cost of education without significant structural changes [10] or adopting more scalable models such as on-line learning [11] or increased use of contingent faculty. Finding answers to these contradictions isn't just a matter of developing sound policies or finding new efficiencies. Rather progress is dependent on clarifying what it means to be educated and the aims society has for, and the rewards it offers, those who pursue higher education, often at personal risk and expense.

Engineering education forms an interesting microcosm of these trends. Right now the STEM — science, technology, engineering, and mathematics — disciplines are the policy darlings of higher education. There are many reasons for this but looking at it from a cynic's perspective it comes down to the fact that every democratically elected politician has to show that their actions created positive change in their district. At the current time technology is driving economic growth [12] and economic growth is thought to create jobs. While engineering is the most expensive undergraduate major to offer on most campuses, it also has among the highest job placement rates, initial salary, and overall return on investment for students [4], [13]. In this environment it is easy to focus too much on the instrumental value of an engineering degree and lose sight of the fact that engineering education is, for most students, the sum total of their college education. The questions that this book seeks to address were discussed in the preface and can be briefly framed as asking what are the moral consequences and responsibilities inherent to educating engineers? A tangential question is to ask what ends does engineering education serves as a means to?

Decades of policy reports have given engineering educators multiple reasons to trumpet their accomplishments and make a strong case for societal investments in engineering education. The conclusion of the Mann report about a century ago [14, p. 118] made the case for:

> "…the modern conception of the professional engineer, not as a conglomerate of classical scholarship and mechanical skill, but as the creator of machine and the interpreter of their human significance, well qualified to increase the materials rewards of human labor and to organize industry for the more intelligent development of men."

Similar reports have been issued at roughly a decennial rate since. A century later in 2018 the opening of the National Academy of Engineering's report *Understanding the Educational and Career Pathways of Engineers* [15] states:

> "Engineering skills and knowledge are foundational to technological innovation and development that drive long-term economic growth and help solve societal challenges. Therefore, to ensure national competitiveness and quality of life it is important to understand and to continuously adapt and improve the educational and career pathways of engineers in the United States."

It is no bad thing to devote one's life to organizing industry or driving long-term economic growth. Yet the reports often quoted by engineering educators frame engineers, and thus the processes used to educate them, as a means to the ends of industrial production or economic growth. What engineering education should be as an end in itself is not clear, or as framed by the philosopher Carl Mitcham [16]: *"Engineering does not provide its own justification for transforming the world, except at the unthinking bottom-line level, or much guidance for what kind of world we should design and construct."* Similarly the human and personal aspects of engineering education often get lost in a more utilitarian focus on jobs and instrumental skills. Given the question of whether engineering education is contributing to moral good, another question explored in this book is what an engineering education might look like if it was considered as an end in itself? The debate over ends vs. means in education is not new; John Henry Newman's classic *The Idea of a University* [17] sought to rebut the utilitarian ideas of John Stuart Mill and Jeremy Bentham.

From the pragmatic, process-oriented stance of engineering such questions may seem overly philosophical since the education of engineers is about both means and ends: what are the most effective means for producing a sufficient number of highly qualified engineers? From this perspective the ends of engineering education are defined through outcomes that can be changed procedurally when needed. While such outcomes are important in engineering education because of current accreditation practices, viewing ends as requirements reflects the current pragmatic and utilitarian views of education rather than personal and civic perspectives. It is also important to ask who determines what the ends should be. *Quis custodiet ipsos custodes?* There is a difference between a government agency or accrediting body seeking to determine the ends of engineering education and the same question being asked by an individual student or faculty member. For the former it is to ensure some standard, and there is some implicit or explicit system of values that underlies setting such standards. For the individual however, the question of ends and means is both personal and philosophical. A student choosing to go into engineering naturally seeks to understand what becoming an engineer entails, that is what the end of all their hard work might be and what opportunity costs come with this choice. Such explorations help student make value-based decisions that guide actions that can ensure a better future for themselves and those they love. Understanding such complex and multifaceted decisions that will permanently affect one's life is a role of personal and practical philosophy.

There is much talk these days of having a personal philosophy. The management and entrepreneurship literature are full of advice on how to craft a personal philosophy that will help you succeed. Academic job seekers often have to craft a statement on their educational philosophy to be considered for a teaching position. Having a personal philosophy seems to help a person accomplish practical ends, but how this is to happen is rarely made clear. Similarly, the term "practical philosophy" may seem self-contradictory since in engineering "philosophical" has come to mean irrelevant or overly theoretical, reflecting the pragmatic epistemic stance of engineers who are trained to address practical problems and ignore information irrelevant to that goal. As described in the previous paragraph here the meaning of personal and practical philosophy is to be able to frame then consider questions that will help an individual live a better life. This definition comes from the work of John Macmurray, a 20th century philosopher who distinguished practical from theoretical philosophy. While theoretical philosophy seeks truth, practical philosophy seeks significance. Significance is what gives life its meaning and although much of our experience fades over time what is significant forms the spine of one's life. To answer questions about how being educated as an engineer can make a life significant this book explores some of the present challenges for engineering education through the lens of Macmurray's system of personal philosophy.

In philosophy the term "personal" does not mean individualized or idiosyncratic. Rather personal refers to a branch of philosophy that emphasizes the importance of the individual. Broadly referred to as personalism, this set of beliefs centers notions of reality on the person by recognizing that individuals have significance, are unique, and serve as ends-in-themselves [18]. Personalism also recognizes that humans exist in relation to other persons and society rather than as isolated rational minds. Compared to some other movements in philosophy there are no luminaries in personalism around which an established school has arisen. Rather there are many thinkers that together form a diffuse collection of thought. Personalism meshes well with practical philosophy since as free agents the important philosophical questions for individuals are related to acting in the world, or questions of morality and ethics.

Morality and ethics are central to the topics this book considers since both engineering and education are facing difficult questions of how to act in the face of uncertainty, and engineering education is where these issues intersect. One issue is how engineering constitutes itself as a profession. Professions establish boundaries [19] which serve not only to define the profession but can exclude people and ideas. The issues of inclusion and equity in engineering are well known, pervasive, and persistent [20]–[22]. Another issue that was discussed in the preface is that engineering has been accused of being complicit in creating and sustaining emerging global challenges in part due its captivity to capitalism [23], [24] which creates ethical challenges [25] for the profession. An epistemological challenge in engineering education is that since engineering knowledge is contingent [26] and heuristic-based [27] increasing rates of knowledge growth and technology development are raising questions about what the core knowledges of engineering are. This epistemological challenge faces education as well since most educational programs are grounded in established disciplines that fiercely preserve their identity while the pressing challenges of the age are better classified as interdisciplinary and convergent. Technology also raises significant questions for education since what is often seen (mistakenly) as the core function of education, knowledge acquisition, can now be done more cheaply through technology. This places educators in the defensive position of asserting that what they do is a fundamentally human endeavor [28] in an age of instrumental utility. Another ethical issue in education is, as discussed previously, the fact that increasing costs of higher education have made it less accessible without taking on significant personal debt while it has become more difficult to thrive in society without a college credential.

This is a book about engineering, education, and engineering education. There are two ways of looking at the intersection of engineering and education, and which perspective one chooses matters greatly in considering a philosophy of engineering education. One is that of a Venn diagram where engineering education sits at the intersection between engineering and education and inherits issues and knowledge from both domains. This approach mirrors the mathematical, positivist framework familiar to engineers who are comfortable with the methods of problem decomposition. By focusing on a narrow enough domain and defining a problem correctly it is possible to decompose the problem into smaller and smaller pieces until the pieces are small enough to solve. Once these issues are solved engineers can then work backwards to assemble the pieces of the puzzle and solve the larger problem. Certain problems—which are often termed simple and complicated [29]—are amenable to this form of solution. A large part of what engineering educators do is teaching students to efficiently adopt this problem-solving methodology.

Looking at the intersection of engineering and education more holistically, such a decomposition approach over-simplifies issues. From the holistic viewpoint engineering education is a wicked problem [30] or challenge with elements that fall into the domain of complexity or chaos [29]. Wicked problems cannot be classified as right or wrong, are understood only in retrospect, have no defined end point, and are unique. For these types of problem decomposition doesn't work because the relevant pieces are highly interconnected and exhibit self-organization and nonlinearity; in other words, they form a complex system. Such systems [31] are not controllable but they are describable. In working with such systems issues can neither be fully understood or controlled since they are dynamic and uncertain. Other methods are needed. In the words of systems expert Donella Meadows [32]:

"We can't find a proper, sustainable relationship to nature, each other, or the institutions we create, if we try to do it from the role of omniscient conqueror... We can't impose our will upon a system. We can listen to what the system tells us, and discover how its properties and our values can work together to bring forth something much better than could ever be produced by our will alone."

From this perspective engineering education is not fully within our control and we must seek to understand the relationship between our values and those expressed by a system influenced by industries, governments, universities, and all the constituents thereof while not losing sight that its purpose is to educate persons. It is in this dynamic relationship, rather than as components of a decomposable mechanism, that individuals and their beliefs and values matter.

As mentioned previously, this book seeks to explore existential issues of engineering education through the work of the 20th century Scottish philosopher John Macmurray. There are several reasons that Macmurray's work can serve as a valuable framework to explore what constitutes good, and what the ends are, in engineering. First, Macmurray contributed greatly to personalism and education is ultimately about persons. Second, he was primarily a practical philosopher. Much of Macmurray's work was not published in academic journals but rather targeted to the public at large, making it broadly approachable[1]. A third reason is that his best-known published works, based on the Gifford Lectures [33], sought to create a philosophical system based on action rather than thought which aligns with the contingent reasoning and underlying epistemic frameworks of engineering. The fact that Macmurray sought to outline a broad philosophical system rather than focus deeply on a specific issue provides the scope needed in addressing a topic as broad as engineering education. If one seeks to develop ethical engineers or identify epistemological challenges in engineering education one branch of philosophy suffices. But in developing a practical philosophy that can inform action one must address questions of what it means to know engineering, act as an engineer, and become an engineer, or in philosophy epistemology, ethics, and ontology. Such breadth requires a systemic view. Finally, Macmurray's philosophy grew out of his belief that society faced a philosophical dilemma in the period between the two world wars as the beliefs of the 19th century no longer served in the 20th. As outlined previously a rationale for this book is the perception of a similar dilemma facing engineering education in the 21st century.

Thoughts on philosophy and engineering education will be developed over the next seven chapters. The second chapter introduces the philosophy of John Macmurray, placing his work in context and exploring concepts of personalism and agency that contribute to the definitions of good and moral action in engineering education. This chapter does not attempt to analyze or critique Macmurray's philosophy relative to others or present an in-depth analysis as other works have done [34]–[36], rather it serves to lay a foundation for development of later ideas. Three shorter chapters then each explore a key element of Macmurray's system. Chapter three explores how persons develop through an iterative process of action and reflection that Macmurray termed the cycle of withdrawal and return. This element of Macmurray's system is the basis for understanding students' development as persons. Chapter four develops ideas around three different modes of reflection, which Macmurray called modes of apperception. The modes of apperception a student learns determine how their experiences build habits that support or limit their opportunities for future action. The fifth chapter explores the principle of the world as one action which connects individuals' actions with the form of society. Since the works of engineers increasingly impact others, the ways of acting they learn as students have societal consequences. With the basis of Macmurray's system to build from, chapter six develops a new, systemic mode of reflection relevant for engineering education. The seventh chapter undertakes a critique of engineering education from the perspective of all four modes of apperception, seeking to broadly and divergently explore the problem space of engineering education and identify how engineering practices and beliefs align with Macmurray's definition of good. The final, eighth chapter brings key ideas together to address the questions of how engineering education can better support moral good and what ends it serves.

2

JOHN MACMURRAY'S PHILOSOPHY OF THE PERSONAL

"What is here proposed is that we substitute the 'I do' for the 'I think' as our starting-point and centre of reference; and do our thinking from the standpoint of action."

John Macmurray, *The Self as Agent*, p. 84.

This chapter adapts and extends the philosophical system developed by the 20th century Scottish philosopher John Macmurray to seek to develop a philosophy to explore the ends towards which engineering education works and how it contributes to good. While Macmurray is well-known by many modern religious thinkers, his work is not widely recognized in academic philosophy circles. Despite his relative obscurity Macmurray's work has great potential to inform new understandings in, or reconceptions of, engineering education, perhaps uniquely so. The goal of this chapter is to introduce the core ideas of Macmurray's system in the context of the life experiences and historical period in which his work arose.

Life and Historical Context

John Macmurrray was born in Scotland just before the start of 20th Century into a devoutly Presbyterian family. This religious upbringing influenced his approach to philosophy which is generally classified as personalism [18] but also as political philosophy [35]. As a young man Macmurray fought in World War I where he served first in the medical corps and later on the front lines in a combat unit where he was severely wounded. Historically the period following the First World War was a period of political, economic, and social upheaval that had strong effects on those who served in the conflict; disillusionment with the societal institutions that let such a conflict occur was widespread. The war effectively ended the power of aristocracies, and led to the rise of socialist and labor movements, women's empowerment, as well as communism and fascism. Macmurray's experiences following the war mirrored those of other returning soldiers and his resulting disillusionment with religious and secular society led him to question traditional methods and approaches to the function of society, driving his development as a philosopher. After the war, Macmurray completed his degree then served in multiple senior academic positions throughout his life including Oxford, University College London, and finally the University of Edinburgh where he stayed until his retirement in 1958. He had a successful academic career, but did not publish in academic journals as much as he gave lectures, wrote books, and became a well-known and followed public figure through the first radio broadcasts on philosophy that he hosted for the BBC in the 1930's and early 1940's [37]. Throughout much of his life he was active politically in various aspects of the socialist and communist movements in Britain and an influential figure in many organizations from the Social Democrats to the Woodcraft Folk.

Macmurray's activism arose from his belief that the political movements of his time—fascism, communism, and corporate capitalism—did not adequately take human worth into account. Both his politics and philosophy critiqued the organic and mechanistic values that underlie these belief systems. While he remained deeply religious throughout his life he did not participate in organized religion until his affiliation with the Society of Friends later in life. An introvert by nature, his deep friendships with many leading thinkers of his day strongly influenced his philosophy. These three elements—the core purpose of religion, the inhumanity of society highlighted by his wartime experiences, and friendship—were to form an individual philosophy that had a strong influence on his professional work [34].

It is difficult to classify Macmurray as a philosopher. His work has a strong spiritual component, yet is based on rational rather than revelational claims and is influenced more by Kant, Marx, and Hegel than Christian thinkers. Most commonly Macmurray is classified with the diffuse philosophical movement known as personalism which focuses on the uniqueness and dignity of individuals [18]. Briefly, personalism developed in the 19th century in reaction to depersonalizing movements in philosophy such as absolute idealism, political movements, and the sense of determinism arising from physics and evolution. Although it draws from a broad spectrum of philosophical movements, personalism puts the person foremost in value and explores personhood through relational or social aspects of what it means to be human. Here person is singular, rather than collective, so that persons are an end in themselves rather than means to a larger social end; there are no ends greater than personhood. Persons are thus not defined as being part of a group nor can they be broken down into component emotions, beliefs, or functions. To be a person is to be unique.

Macmurray is also classified as a humanist and his major work clearly aligns with humanist views of human value and agency as well as a critical approach to religion. Others classify Macmurray as an idealist since his view of humanity maintains that idealism is necessary as the basis of correct action. He was also active in political organizations, and due to his work in this area some authors highlight his contributions to political philosophy [35]. Despite his relative obscurity in academic philosophy, there has recently been a Macmurray revival. In 1996 the British politician Tony Blair wrote the introduction to *The Personal World* [36], the first collection of Macmurray's selected works. A special issue of the *Oxford Review of Education* focused on Macmurray [38], and the John Macmurray Fellowship [39] supports occasional conferences focusing on his work.

The breadth of Macmurray's work classifies him as a systematic thinker who was interested in the broader application of philosophy to human society. Over the course of his life he developed a philosophy based on thought being secondary and in service to action much in the way that some claim (incorrectly) that engineering instantiates the discoveries of science. For Macmurray theory and practice are inseparable [40, p. 21]:

"There is of necessity and interplay, in all human activities, between theory and practice. It is characteristic of Man that he solves his practical problems by taking thought; and all his theoretical activities have their origins, at least, in his practical requirements."

His action-based philosophical system is outlined in the Gifford Lectures [34] and later published as two books, *The Self as Agent* [40] and *Persons in Relation* [41]. In these books Macmurray lays out many of the major ideas that were his life's work, ideas that can better inform how we can educate engineers to face complex human challenges in the coming decades. The values and rationale on which these books were based were developed earlier in a series of radio presentations on philosophy broadcast on the BBC in the early 1930's. These broadcasts, later published as *Freedom in the Modern World* [42], were aimed at a non-specialist audience and were, to the surprise of many in the broadcasting industry, quite popular since they addressed contemporary societal issues.

Underlying Values:
Faith, Freedom, Reality, and Morality

The basis of Macmurray's radio presentations was his belief that life in the 1930's presented a dilemma between holding on to the societal values of the 19th century that had resulted in the First World War or crafting a new philosophy that could guide life in the 20th century. The root of this dilemma arose from society overvaluing rational thought while not paying sufficient attention to persons' emotional development [42, p. 47]; the integration of intellectual and emotional life is central to Macmurray's philosophy. While in Western thought emotion is often viewed as the polar opposite of reason, Macmurray focused on their synergy. Emotion serves as the motive force for action and the guide to what our intellect seeks to achieve. If we are to value things that are good and just then our emotions must be up to this task, so our emotional development is as important as our rational development. Just as the Enlightenment replaced religious authority with authority derived from an individual's reason, Macmurray saw the need for modern society to recognize the authority of our emotional capacities 42, p. 52]:

> "We are standing, to-day, at the second crisis of our European history; the second great crisis in which we chose, after much fear and hesitation, and persecution, to trust one another to think for ourselves and to stand by the expression of our honest thought. Now we are called upon to implement that faith in the human mind by trusting in the integrity of human feeling."

In his BBC radio broadcasts Macmurray took his audience on a journey that addressed *"the fundamental issues facing any real philosophy…a diagnosis of the philosophical problem presented by contemporary life."* [42, p. 15]. The role of philosophy, which has both theoretical and practical components, is to understand the inner significance of one's life which depends both on emotion and intellect. For Macmurray the role of theoretical philosophy is to separate the real from the unreal in life while practical philosophy is concerned with how to make one's life significant. In discussing what makes life real and significant Macmurray consistently returns to four central concepts: faith, freedom, reality, and morality. Each of these, described below, can be thought of as qualities, that arise both from the person and their environment, which an individual needs to understand and address if they wish to live a life that has significance.

Faith: Macmurray's use of the term faith reflects the importance he places on the role of an individual's emotional life. In the 1930's when Macmurray produced his BBC lectures the issues facing society were economic woes and the conflicting political systems of capitalism, communism, socialism, and fascism. Macmurray recognized that these larger issues impacted upon the beliefs of individuals, just as existential issues like climate change do today. The senseless tragedy of the First World War had undermined many people's faith in the ideas upon which society was grounded, and the resulting mistrust in societal institutions led to people lacking faith in themselves and their own beliefs. While the term faith is usually affiliated with religious conviction it is one of several terms that are used outside normal contexts in Macmurray's writings. To Macmurray faith provided individuals with a sense of what they valued and thus what created meaning in their lives. Without being able to identify what one values, a person's intellectual and emotional lives become disconnected. Thus a goal of Macmurray's philosophy was to provide elements of a modern faith, or principles which allows individuals to find value in their lives however they chose to live them. Faith is the center of, and stems from, the emotional life which provides one a sense of what is good and worthwhile. If one's emotional life is lacking or based on unreality it is impossible to have the faith that guides day-to-day actions.

<u>Freedom</u>: If an individual has faith they have reasons for acting but in order to act they also need the freedom to do so. Macmurray identifies three types of freedom that lead to different conceptions of moral action which appear throughout his work: material, organic, and personal. Nonliving matter obeys natural laws and is free to act according to these laws but cannot act outside them. Organic or living matter additionally has the freedom to adapt to the larger environment with each organism a tiny part of the continual adaptation of life generally on the planet. The third type of freedom is personal freedom which is a person's ability to develop into who they really are or spontaneously reflect their own nature. The moral notions derived from each of these forms of freedom are discussed subsequently. A person's freedom is limited when they are overly constrained in their material, social, or personal lives. Macmurray does not imply that constraints do not or should not exist, but that the individual should have sufficient freedom to be able to undertake meaningful intellectual and emotional development within these constraints[2]. Freedom in the personal life enables us to grow into who we are, freedom in the social life lets us live spontaneously in our community, and freedom in the material life means we are not too inhibited in our potential. For Macmurray freedom is the central question of practical philosophy since without

freedom and the spontaneity that it supports it is not possible to construct a meaningful life. The centrality of freedom in Macmurray's work has similarities with the political philosophies of Paolo Friere [43], Cesar Chavez, and Ivan Illich [44]. Freedom is also related to Lonergan's conception of willing since to exercise will requires freedom [45]. It is technologies ability to provide or limit such freedoms that engineering intersects Macmurray's notions of good.

<u>Reality</u>: The concept of reality is the focus of theoretical philosophy, and Macmurray relates individuals' capacity for freedom to how well they conceive of the reality they live in. Unreality in our intellectual life means we have reduced our freedom to act since we choose ineffective means to achieve our objectives. Unreality in our emotional lives means we aim our efforts at the wrong end and our actions wind up being emotionally unsatisfactory. Understanding reality is thus vital to survival and societies that fail to understand reality—the French monarchy before the terror, the Czars before the Bolshevik revolution, and perhaps us at the cusp of climate change—do not survive. Reality is a difficult concept since what we think determines our reality, not just what we profess to be true. For Macmurray realness is more important than truth because our perceived reality is based on what we see as significant. We pay attention to that which is significant to ourselves and overlook the insignificant; a fact that is true but insignificant does not form part of our reality at this point in time although it may later if it takes on significance. Significance is related to faith because without finding value in our lives our actions lack significance and life takes on a sense of unreality [42, p. 113]:

> "There were times when we really lived, and really got at the meaning of life. There are beliefs which we have retained, which experience has tested for us, and which we acknowledge as truth. There are actions which we are proud to have performed, and which we wish to repeat because they were just right. These are the significant things in our experience, the real things, the important things."

The sources of unreality in our intellectual life arise from errors in thinking, and in our emotional lives through misplacing significance. Macmurray argues that a role of philosophy is to guard against these errors through testing our beliefs through experience in the world and comparing our experience to that of others. To compare our experience with others we must be real ourselves if we are to represent our beliefs accurately and get meaningful feedback. It is through meaningful sharing with others that we learn our beliefs are right in some cases and wrong in others; being wrong arms us with skepticism. The danger is that if we become too skeptical we start to believe in nothing, lose faith, focus our attention internally, and so drift into unreality. Macmurray highlights three paths to unreal thinking: making up unreal scenarios in our own mind, over-generalizing (becoming too intellectual), and disconnecting our thought from action so we never receive external feedback. We can similarly have unreality in our emotional lives. Since emotion reflects our ability to perceive worth, it is our feelings that drive our motives for action. Macmurray posits that our emotional life is as ordered as our intellectual life, but on different principles[3]. As with the intellect we are unreal in our feelings when we become disconnected from reality and focus inwardly rather than connecting emotionally with others. There is a difference, however, between connecting emotionally to others and having our emotions be stimulated by external events. While external events can arouse emotion in us Macmurray classifies these as unrealities in our emotional lives[4]. In summary unreality—in thought or feeling—arises from being focused inwardly and living one's life for oneself rather than others. We become real by focusing our reason and emotion outwardly and connecting with other persons. The need to connect to others to be real ourselves is a central theme in Macmurray's work.

Morality: With faith, freedom, and a grounding in reality individuals have the motive, ability, and perceptiveness to act, but to act rightly they need a sense of morality. Morality in essence gives us guidelines on how to act to be the best we can be in a word in which our actions affect others. Because freedom is required for personal development a moral action is one that supports, rather than inhibits, freedom. The question of morality then is to act in a way that can enable personal development for ourselves and others. The different forms of freedom—material, organic, and personal— which serve as models for society also are used by Macmurray as the basis for different models of morality. Macmurray calls moral systems that are adapted from understandings of material freedom *mechanical* morality since they frame morality through obedience to a moral law. Such moral systems are mechanical in that they seek uniformity and predictability in human behavior which allows for better societal planning but treat humans as if they are material objects. Macmurray is unwavering that obedience does not serve freedom and is not a valid basis for a system of morality.

A second form of morality arises from adapting models of organic freedom in which individual organisms' role is to support the web of life. Given that the human environment is society, in this system morality is defined by working toward social good, or a morality of service. Macmurray argues that *"...a morality of service and self-sacrifice to the community is a denial of human reality. It treats everybody as a means to an end."* (*ibid*, p. 199). Furthermore, such morality lets those who decide the form of society dictate others' freedom. The utilitarian focus of engineering education often aligns with organic forms of morality.

The third form of moral good is personal morality which consists of being who we really are and having the freedom to express that to others. This form of morality relies on faith, freedom, and reality that Macmurray summarizes as (*ibid*, p. 209):

> "Morality is the expression of personal freedom. That freedom is grounded in our capacity to be real and to love reality. The supreme reality of human life is the reality of persons, and of persons in personal relation with one another. Friendship, therefore, is the essence of morality...Ultimately our own reality consists precisely in our ability to know people as they really are and to love them for what they really are.

Everything that prevents that—fear or pride or the passion for wealth or power or position in men, the insubordination of human beings to organizations and institutions, an unjust distribution of wealth or opportunity in the community— everything that opposes or denies the inherent right of a human individual to be himself and to realize and love the reality of other human beings, is the enemy of morality."

Each of these concepts—faith, freedom, reality, and morality—have an inherent dualism, or dialectic nature. This dualism is established on a love–fear spectrum that is central to Macmurray's philosophical system. Love is expressed by freedom in action and spontaneity. On the other hand *"Fear freezes the spontaneity of life. The more fear there is in us, the less alive we are. Fear accomplishes this destruction of life by turning us in upon ourselves and so isolating us from the work outside us."* (*ibid*, p. 59). Each of these four concepts has an aspect based on love or fear which Macmurray defines as positive or negative: freedom – constraint, faith – doubt, reality – unreality, and morality – isolation.

Macmurray borrowed from Hegel and perhaps Marx in using dialectics in his writing [36, ch. 3]. The terms positive and negative form such a dialectic. The tensions between these poles produce new insights and for Macmurray the tensions that arise in the love – fear dialectic are one of the engines that help drive an individual's development as a person. Understanding dialectics is a key concept in Macmurray's work since, as will be discussed later, no person is characterized by only positive or negative relationships. Love and fear are within all of us to one degree or another and it is the way we iteratively resolve the inherent tensions between these points of view that determine who we are and how we act. Which emotion predominates in our relationships, love (positive) or fear (negative), depends both on our prior relationships and how we reflect on those relationships. In other words, relationships, like our growth as a person, are iterative and developmental.

From the standpoint of exploring a philosophy of engineering education that derives from Macmurray's work, the four qualities of faith, freedom, reality, and morality serve as guideposts to the broader aims of education. While there are specific ways of knowing, acting, and being that come from being educated as an engineer, underlying all forms of education is the central element of growing as a person. Macmurray claims that it is by seeking to develop these qualities in ourselves that we grow as persons and the extent to which they are developed influence how we use the other knowledge and skills we gain. As described in the next section, we develop these qualities by acting in the world.

MacMurray's Philosophical System: The Gifford Lectures

The most complete framing of Macmurray's philosophical system is his Gifford Lectures given in 1952 and 1953 and published as The *Self as Agent* [40] and *Persons in Relation* [41]. The Gifford Lectures, given at four Scottish universities—the universities of Edinburgh, Glasgow, St. Andrews and Aberdeen—are prestigious lectures on natural theology that have included a wide range of perspectives including those of William James, Alfred North Whitehead, Neils Bohr, Hanna Arendt, Karl Barth, and Carl Sagan. Macmurray's Gifford Lectures tie many threads of his work in philosophy together into one system [34]. In his Gifford Lectures Macmurray undertakes a broad systematic foray to develop a form of personalism that spans much of human experience. The lectures broadly outline a personal tangent to Western philosophy which Macmurray saw as too mechanistic or organic. Macmurray saw his work an incomplete sketch rather than rigorous and complete, and his hope was others would follow and further develop his system.

The tangent taken by Macmurray is the "form of the personal" which is distinguished from the form of *mechanical* (logical) or *organic* (romantic) thought addressed by previous philosophers. By developing a philosophy of the personal Macmurray sought to extend the boundaries of scientific and rational thought to encompass human emotions and endeavors which rely on emotion, such as art and the humanities, so they could be given the same considerations as rational thought. Like philosophical systems such as Stoicism [46] Macmurray sought to develop ideas on what a "good life" for the individual means. Macmurray builds his system from a Western philosophical tradition that values individuals by starting with the claim that a philosophy of the personal must start with a view of a person as an agent capable of action that creates change in the world rather than a rational, disembodied mind. We are formed not from how we think, but from actions that elicit a response both from the world at large as well as those who inhabit it. This framing is close to the philosophies of Martin Buber and Gabriel Marcel, both friends of Macmurray; of the three Macmurray tried to make sense of how the personal was to function as a philosophic system [34].

Macmurray bases his philosophy of the personal on Kant's *Critiques* since he viewed the *Critiques* as the most adequate philosophy for tackling a range of problems related to resolving scientific, religious, and romantic thought. Kant wrote the *Critiques* in a time where there were many conflicting issues and ideas. The skepticism introduced by Descartes' *A Discourse on the Method* [47] raised a rational challenge to traditional authority and led to a rational and mechanical philosophy centered on the mind as highlighted by Descartes' dictum *Cogito Ergo Sum* (I think therefore I am). The later development of empiricism by British philosophers such as Hume introduced a practical or sense-based view of reason but failed to account for emotional and religious (moral) aspects of human life. Kant in his *Critiques* created a systematic philosophy that reconciled these issues. Macmurray builds from Kant due to the systematic approach and the fact that the *Critiques* are the departure point for much subsequent Western philosophy.

For Macmurray the keystone of Kant's Critical Philosophy is the "thing-in-itself" or duality between the noumenal (ideal, abstracted, existing independent of human perception) and phenomenal (experienced, known through the senses) worlds. For Kant the thing-in-itself was necessary to free will but Macmurray is critical of the noumenal-phenomenal dualism since the failure to align the theoretical (noumenal) and practical (phenomenal) aspects of reason leaves the person split between theoretical (self-as-knowing) and practical (self-as-sensing). Additionally, because of this dualism Kant's philosophy fails to adequately capture idealist and moral aspects of human life.

Macmurray's first criticism of Kant is that we must exist in the noumenal (theoretical) world to have free will so that we can act morally (from duty). The issue is that since this world is not knowable an end to our action cannot be determined. Action occurs in the phenomenal (practical) world to achieve a given end, and our actions in fact change this world. Macmurray argues that we can't live in two worlds at the same time if moral good is practically possible and therefore rejects Kant's dualism on the basis that if moral action is to be real it has to actually be done in the world through action which is knowable. Macmurray's second criticism is that while Kant could critique reason he could not critique morality because starting from Descartes' "I think" focuses on the self rather than relations with others which Macmurray defines as the basis of moral action. In other words, reason is essentially a first person view while morality and religion are second person perspectives. Macmurray argues that the central issue with the theoretical – practical duality is the assumption that being and thought are an identity.

From this second criticism Macmurray outlines several theoretical issues inherent to Western philosophy he seeks to address in his system. First, a philosophy that starts from Cogito results in a dualism of theory and practice since while action can be conceived of, its effect on the purely theoretical world always remains a mystery. Second, the focus on thought and the theoretical world in philosophy has led to underlying societal narratives that are predominantly egotistical and theoretical. Macmurray asks how can we actually live both in the noumenal world that exists independent of my perception and a phenomenal world I know I can change? Additionally, he sees a disembodied rational mind as egocentric, focusing on solely the "I" rather than the "You", a viewpoint that does not sufficiently value the personal relationships through which moral action can be known. Furthermore, while Descartes' systematic process of doubt can serve as a rational basis for belief Macmurray claims that the isolated, egotistical nature of a disembodied mind can err on the side of doubting too much with the practical consequence of eliminating potential good from the world. In other words, human endeavors that claim to derive from rationality are prone to lead to too much doubt (or in statistics type two errors), denying the existence of factors important to human thriving.

Practically Macmurray viewed this dualism, which has been deeply ingrained in modern Western thought, as a key issue for modern society and human freedom due to his perception of a widening contradiction between science and morality that had both individual and societal consequences. In brief, moral choice relies upon individual freedom since one must be free to act in a way that is right. Knowing what is right to do, however, is an internal, subjective conviction; just because an individual is convinced they are right does mean their convictions are aligned with moral good. It is not possible to turn to science and other mechanistic (positivist) philosophies to learn how to act for the good since they are ultimately deterministic, i.e., discover what already exists. Action by its very nature determines the future; Macmurray summarizes this tension as *"We can only know a determinate world; we can only act in an indeterminate world."* [40, p. 55]. Although purely practical (phenomenal) reason provides the ability to act in the world, without some ideal of good arising from the noumenal world reason by itself cannot ensure a person's actions will make the world better. Imagine, for example, a leader who imagines some notion of the good then compels others into accepting this notion as the end towards which society works. The leader can apply practical reason to achieve the envisioned end by creating a romantic ideal of the end then using technology to develop ever-better methods to achieve it. Such single-minded focus on an ideal ultimately limits human freedom. Macmurray saw the effects of this dualism acted out in the world in the rise of Nazi Germany.

In building his philosophical system Macmurray resolves the theory-practice dualism by rejecting Descartes' *cogito ergo sum* (I think therefore I am) and conceives of humans as agents (actors) rather than thinkers. The rejection of Descartes' viewpoint of humans as a rational, disembodied mind forms the lynchpin of Macmurray's system. His personalist philosophy is based on thinking of persons as agents who have the ability to act to change the world as well as to learn how to act for good. To Descartes knowledge starts in doubt and ends in certainty. Macmurray rejects this and places belief before doubt since belief (faith) is a necessary emotional catalyst for action. Thus Macmurray's work frames action as primary and thinking as secondary and resulting from action. The focus on action is a second lynchpin in Macmurray's system.

Macmurray's focus on action over thought and rejection of a practical-theoretical dualism has appeal as a foundation from which to explore a philosophy of engineering education since engineering in many ways serves as a bridge between the phenomenal and noumenal worlds. While science and mathematics seek to develop ways to obtain insights into the noumenal world, engineering draws from these scientific insights and "reverses the vector of abstraction" [48] in order to use theoretical knowledge for changing human experience in the phenomenal or practical world. A sense-limited human, for example, can't perceive the entire physical reality of a jet engine because some pieces get in the way of others and the overall performance depends on material properties we cannot directly sense. However we can represent this reality through an exploded diagram of engine or the results of x-ray testing of the turbine blades, for example. Engineering understanding depends on representations, as Schopenhauer's critique of Kant [49] suggested. Such representations blur the lines between the phenomenal and noumenal worlds but tend to reflect the physical and not the personal world. Practically the phenomenal-noumenal divide expresses itself through theoretical-practical debates in engineering education that affect the order of courses in a curriculum, the debate about the relative importance of technical vs. professional skills, or math and science prerequisites to engineering courses. The dualism

Macmurray seeks to address—that the real world is theoretical and exists independent of my perception but as an engineer I can change the world for the better—is a central tension in engineering education.

Macmurray is aware that it is no small matter to break with foundational ideas in Western philosophy. The *Self as Agent* laid out how a philosophy based on action avoids the contradiction between viewing the self as a thinker, an idea which goes back at least as far as Plato, and the self as an agent. In brief, acting implies that one has *thought* about what action to take; thought is inherent to and implied by action. In this view thought determines true from false while action determines right from wrong; there is no real moral choice without action. Starting with the centrality of action Macmurray lays out four characteristics of a person which guide the development of his philosophy of personal agency [44, pp. 100-103]:

- The self exists only as an agent. The agentic individual (self-as-agent) acts in the world (Other) and thus is a person with both physical and mental faculties.
- The Cartesian view of an individual—a rational, disembodied mind—(self-as-subject) is subsumed within the self-as-agent and is not separable.
- The self-as-subject serves the self-as-agent since all knowledge arises from the individual's reflection on their actions and such knowledge exists to determine future action.
- The self-as-subject and self-as-agent do not form a duality; both are necessary to each other since action and knowledge form a unity.

Macmurray was often criticized for his loose use of language [34] by defining terms that are subject to multiple interpretations. Here the term *agent* describes the person in the mode of action or engaging with the world (which Macmurray termed the Other) while *subject* refers to the person in the mode of reflection, standing isolated from the world as a rational observer in Descartes' tradition. The agent engages with the world not just visually, a sense mode that implies disengaged observation, but more holistically through touch and feelings. I am more in the mode of subject when I grade, while I am in the mode of agent when I teach.

In other words, to act the agent must "push" against what exists, see how it pushes back, and seek to understand this resistance both rationally and emotionally. There is no subject-object duality in action; an agent in action is both subject and object in an almost Newtonian sense because the Other always reacts in some way to an agent's actions. Rephrased in more engineering terminology, the agent is an integral component of any system to which they belong and the system can't be described independently of understanding the agent's role within that system.

Macmurray thus claims that all of us are simultaneously a subject and agent, doer and thinker. For Macmurray "I do" integrally includes "I think"; I must know the Other to be able to act upon it (see the concept of reality discussed previously). However not any knowing or knowledge suffices to inform action; knowledge is valued in relation to intention. At the moment of acting the agent makes a choice, informed by the information available to them, about which action will best achieve the outcome they desire. Effective action is neither random nor spontaneous, to consistently act correctly requires the agent develop habits through practice. While such repetition is key in education, e.g., homework problems or studying for a test, developing the habits needed for action is not synonymous with acquiring skills or knowledge associated with a way of acting. While knowledge *may* be useful to action, the value of any given knowledge is only determined through acting, thus making knowledge personal, i.e., knowing. Knowledge and action are distinguished temporally; action generates a past by actualizing a possibility and the knowing gained from this process illuminates possible future actions. Action only exists in the present since the past is determinate (and thus knowable) and the future is indeterminate; it is what we do now that matters. Thus both the usefulness of knowledge and development of habit are determined through action that make future possibilities more likely. Through acting we directly confront questions of right and wrong that both refine our knowledge and develop habits. The experience of acting is fundamentally different than the experience of practicing; practice may help develop habits, but it does not have the moral implications of acting. Macmurray points out that it is through acting that we address the immediate question of "How can I do what is right?" rather than the distal question of "How can I know what is right to do?"

Moral Implications of Macmurray's System

The term "moral" often has religious connotations, particularly evangelical associations, which make many secular readers uncomfortable. Morals, however, are simply standards of behavior that determine ways that are or are not acceptable for a person to act. The term moral is from the Latin *moralis*, "pertaining to manners". This section discusses the moral implications of Macmurray's system and explores how philosophy can help engineering educators determine what is right to do. When we act it is not just against an inanimate Other but being human means we all exist within a field of other agents who affect our actions as we affect theirs. The fact that we are in relationships with other agents is a central tenet of Macmurray's philosophy that separates it from Cartesian focused perspectives and also defines what constitutes a moral action. For Macmurray the fact that we act within a network of other agents, persons, is the central fact of human existence and his system seeks to develop a philosophy that supports satisfactory (moral) ends when the agent acts in a field of other agents. In brief, if an agent is to act for both satisfactory and moral ends (the good of others) they must base their actions on a philosophy that values other persons. In developing these aspects of his system Macmurray makes several assumptions:

- Due to the strong influence of other agents on our actions, the individual unit of humanity is not an isolated, rational mind rather it is persons in relation with each other. This assertion distinguishes Macmurray's system since its implications are contrary to many core values of individualistic, Western thought.
- A corollary is that Descartes' view of humans as an isolated, rational mind does not qualify as fully a human existence.

- Human relationships are not a means to an end, although they have elements of a means; rather satisfactory relations with others exist as an end to themselves.
- Humans are defined by their actions, and actions always occur in relation to others.

In developing his philosophy of the personal Macmurray parallels ideas from Martin Buber who defined two types of human relationships [50]. Those categorized as "I-It" are based on experiences that allow us to classify objects into categories and act towards them as a member of that category. In contrast "I-Thou" relationships are holistic, intersubjective, and deeply relational in ways that potentially transform both parties.

Macmurray claims that the relational nature of human existence starts at birth since as humans we are born into a mother-child relationship that serves as an end in itself as well as, for the child, a means to the end of survival. Human beings survive not on instinct but by being helpless, and this helplessness builds the need for relationship into our core being. If an infant were to develop without human contact, then his or her actions could be attributed to a core rational being in the Cartesian sense. However numerous case studies show that both human children and primates who develop without such relations have great difficulties throughout adult life [51], [52]. While our first relation is with a caregiver, over time our relations expand to a web of personal relationships (family), and we learn to perceive that our actions against a non-animate Other should be different than those against other agents. Over time we learn three different modes of action: treating the Other as personal (another agent), treating the Other as inanimate stuff (not agent), and a middle, indeterminate category that can applies to other forms of life; for example, we may eat beef but build a long-term relationship with a pet. As we grow, we develop different types of relations with other agents that include direct relationships where we interact with other agents directly and indirect relationships where our actions affect those we don't know. Indirect relations are impersonal, where we see the other person through an instrumental or rational lens, for example as a means to an end.

Just like Macmurray's foundational concepts of faith, freedom, reality, and faith relationships have a dialectic nature since they are broadly based on either love or fear. In Macmurray's writings love is used often synonymously with the term *positive*. Positive actions are ones in which the agent acts in concert with the Other or action taken for benefit of another agent. Positive actions or emotions are heterocentric, or focused outward. For Macmurray love is equated with life and is outwards facing, action-oriented, and spontaneous rather than mechanical or calculated. On the other hand, the term fear or *negative* is used when an agent sees the Other as a resistance to her will that she must act against. In actions involving another agent, fear is egocentric and can take the form of fear for oneself or the fear of another. Individuals whose lives are dominated by fear are focused inwardly and express the fear through individualism, selfishness, being defensive, or pretense which Macmurray associated with characteristics of the isolated Cartesian self.

While the social sciences have focused on the relational nature of human existence, historically such relationships have not been emphasized in engineering education. This is changing, however, as engineering education becomes more design focused [53]. Many of the relationships engineers have with the larger public is through the products they design. While these relationships have traditionally been indirect the increasing focus on user-centered and human-centered design captures some elements of direct and personal relationships. The importance of such relationships to engineering education is explored in subsequent chapters.

Summary

This chapter has outlined elements central to Macmurray's philosophy necessary to further develop three major ideas of Macmurray's system that will be explored in depth in the next chapters. All education, engineering or otherwise, is based on underlying values. For Macmurray these are faith, freedom, reality, and morality all of which are defined in terms of the person and their relations with other persons. Education also implicitly or explicitly includes notions of development of the self and its capabilities. For Macmurray such development occurs through action. Macmurray's philosophy is in many respects an educational philosophy that places human development central to moral good. As he states at the conclusion of *Freedom in the Modern World*: "*Self realization is the true moral ideal.*" (p. 219). His work also aligns with other educational philosophers although he does not acknowledge these contributions in his own work. The emphasis on focusing externally and learning from experience draws from American pragmatism as laid forth by Charles Pierce, William James, and John Dewey [54]–[56]. Macmurray's approach also aligns with the contextual, situated beliefs of engineers which rely on heuristics for their work [27]. The focus on community, and testing one's beliefs in friendship with others, aligns with the liberal education ideas articulated by Cardinal Newman [17] although Macmurray and Newman view the role and function of religion quite differently. In terms of educational philosophies [57], Macmurray aligns with a learner centered perspective since he posits that the best future for humans is to develop all individuals' capacity for freedom through creating community and friendships rather than through managed social or educational programs.

It is easy to misinterpret Macmurray's philosophy as utopian given its focus on ideals such as freedom and reality. Macmurray recognizes, however, that these ideals are never fully achieved but rather each person must actively work towards them through a dialectic and developmental process. The freedom to develop as a unique person rather than as part of a collective is what truly matters; this quest is long, difficult, and requires seeking deep truths that can only be mutually developed in meaningful friendships. In this Macmurray stands with Newman in opposition to more utilitarian notions of education since while a focus on the utility of education produces benefits for society, for the individual it comes at the cost of focusing too much on trivial questions – what should I do rather than who should I be?

The fact that Macmurray's philosophy is practical and action-focused, arises from a perceived societal dilemma, addresses both interobjective and intersubjective reality, and defines moral good based on benefits to persons gives it a significant number of intersections with many ideas in engineering education. In today's world we too face dilemmas but rather than the Great Depression and the rise of fascist and communist regimes they are issues related to the roles of capitalism and financialization, environmental degradation, economic inequities, social injustices, and rising authoritarianism. Engineering plays a role in all these societal issues. It is unclear if engineering education can effectively contribute to addressing these concerns if we model ourselves after yesterday's engineer [58]. Thus at some level our dilemma is the same addressed by Macmurray back in the 1930's; what worked for us in the past will not work in the future and we must develop some basis for how to act differently than we have in the past. The challenges going forward for engineering education are not just matters of learning or organizational science, rather what are we going to do with that science, and how it can create the kind of world that will make human life significant.

The next three chapters expand upon concepts central to Macmurray's system: the iterative nature of a person's development (*the cycle of withdrawal and return*), how our ways of reflecting on our actions determine how we come to perceive and act in the world (*modes of apperception*), and the way our actions come to affect other persons and the world at large (*the theory of the world as one action*). Each of these concepts contributes to a framework on which the later critique of engineering education is built.

3
ACTION AND REFLECTION – THE RHYTHM OF WITHDRAWAL AND RETURN

"All meaningful knowledge is for the sake of action,
and all meaningful action for the sake for friendship."

MacMurray, *The Self as Agent*, p. 17

As outlined in the previous chapter John Macmurray's philosophy centers on how we come to be persons. In his system a person's development occurs over time through their experience of acting in the world. Since acting is primary to knowing an agent learns about the world through their actions and knowledge arises from the actions the agent performs. In his work Macmurray describes the iterative nature of becoming a person, which occurs continuously through our day-to-day actions which inform us about the world and our relationship to others.

Because he viewed persons as continually engaging in actions then withdrawing to reflect on the results of their actions Macmurray named the development of knowledge through action *the rhythm of withdrawal and return*. Phrased for education Macmurray's learning cycle is based on the supposition that following an agent's action they withdraw to reflect on what they did, gain new knowledge through reflection, and then return to action by using that knowledge to formulate new approaches to gain their intention. To Macmurray being human is defined iteratively through action that is reflectively informed by knowledge gained through prior action. It is thus action, rather than knowledge which is primary in our development since it is through our actions that we both come to know the world and develop habits of action and reflection. This model aligns with Dewey's pragmatic view of education [56].

Macmurray described the cycle of withdrawal and return in detail in *The Self as Agent* [40]. As engineering often communicates in graphical representations, Macmurray's description is represented here as a six-step iterative cycle shown in Figure 3.1. At the center of this cycle are the Self (agent) and the Other the agent acts upon. Macmurray's use of the term Other encompasses both actions that change the physical world or actions involving other agents (persons). The upper three parts of the cycle corresponds to acting and the lower part to knowing and/or knowledge (depending on how much the agent draws from her own or others' experience). The cycle of acting (return) and knowing (withdrawal) takes place sequentially in time as shown by the oval surrounding the Self and Other. The three steps in the action part of the cycle are on the upper part of the oval and the three reflection steps on the lower part. Each of these steps and their interrelations are more fully explained below.

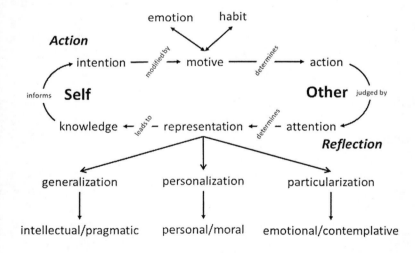

Figure 3.1: *The cycle of withdrawal and return as outlined in* The Self as Agent *modified to show the personal mode introduced in* Persons in Relation.

Intention: Action begins when the agent has an intention to act against the Other to achieve some desired outcome. The intention is to change the Other, and thus the future, in a way that is desirable to the agent. The agent's intention is always conscious and derived from their knowledge of the Other. Intention is causal, that is it is forward looking into the future and the action the agent takes is intended to cause a change in the future state of the Other. As the neurosurgeon James Doty describes in *Into the Magic Shop* [59], intention can serve as more than simply intent and fundamentally affects the way we perceive the world.

Motive: The agent's intention is affected by their anticipation of the outcome of their action. While the agent may wish for a particular outcome, it may or may not be realized depending on the effectiveness of the agent's action. Anticipation necessarily involves elements of feeling, so the agent's intention is modified by their motive [44, pp. 194-197]. While intention is conscious and what the agent seeks to accomplish, the underlying emotion—either fear (negative) or love (positive)—affects the intended action. Motive acts as the (usually) unconscious emotional filter to conscious intention. We are generally not aware of our motive since we focus our attention outwardly on our goal rather than inwardly on our emotions. In Macmurray's system motives arise through emotion or habit as shown in Figure 3.1. The emotional aspect of motive originates in a person's relationships since as persons we rely on others' actions for our own well-being; i.e., others help to determine our emotional state. The habitual aspect of motive arises when an agent has performed an action so many times that the habit serves as a mostly unconscious motive.

Action: The agent then has a choice of how to perform the action to change the Other. What choice the agent makes depends on factors embedded in the cycle such as intention, motive, the anticipated outcomes, and what knowledge they have of ways to act. While there is a choice of possible actions, the agent must commit to one and then actually act. Following the moment of action the agent begins the next part of the cycle, withdrawing into the self and starting the reflective phase of the cycle.

Attention: The intent of the agent and their anticipation of achieving a given outcome determines how the agent pays attention to the effects of their action. Choice of attention is necessary since human beings are not omniscient; we must choose which outcomes of our actions to observe. A corollary is that our actions have effects that are effectively invisible since we do not pay attention to them. If we acted with different intention or based on different knowledge our attention might focus in another direction and we would view the results of our action in a different light. The agent's focus of attention at the moment following action thus serves as a pivot point in the turn from action to reflection.

Representation: By focusing attention on some results of the action the agent constructs a mental representation—i.e., schema [60] or mental model—of the relation between the intention and results of the action. The process of constructing a representation or reflecting on the act is what enables the agent to transfer their experience to knowledge. Macmurray, drawing from Kant, uses the outdated term "mode of apperception" to identify three different ways agents construct such representations. The first representational path labeled "generalization" in Figure 3.1 is that characterized by science where specifics or particulars of the Other are ignored and the agent generalizes the result of the action such that the representation can apply to a broad class of Other. This mode aligns well with dominant belief systems in engineering. The path labeled "particularization" focuses on unique particulars, epitomized by art, to create as detailed and accurate a representation of the specific Other at the moment that the action occurred and captures elements of emotion. The third path, labeled "personal" is where the agent seeks to understand the effect on other persons and whether the action contributed to their freedom and community. Modes of apperception are discussed in detail in the next chapter.

Knowledge: Regardless of the approach used, the agent's creation or refinement of a representation leads to knowledge. Knowledge modifies the agent's understanding of themselves and the Other and enables them to conceive of new courses of action or modify their intention. Adding to the agent's knowledge in a way that enables further action shifts back to the action part of the cycle. By iteratively repeating the cycle new knowledge enables the agent to return to action, refine the means or target of his/her action, and thereby better fulfill his/her intention and realize the anticipated results.

Unlike the Cartesian view of an isolated, rational mind the cycle of withdrawal and return encompasses both thinking and feeling. An act is defined as the realization of an agent's intention and both the start and end of the act are defined through the agent's feelings. The start of an act is associated with a feeling of dissatisfaction that provides the rationale to act; the agent's valuation of this feeling determines both whether an action occurs and which action occurs. The agent's choice of action arises through prior reflection which allows a set of possibilities for action to be seen in the Other. By anticipating a result that aligns with their intention the agent selects the most valued of these possibilities to act upon. For humans, anticipation is selective so the choice to act eliminates, at least at a given time, other avenues of action. Thus emotional valuations, which Macmurray terms faith, affect the choice of what action to take, which in turn affects the cycle of Figure 3.1. Emotion also affects the end of the action since the agent will feel some level of satisfaction or dissatisfaction depending on whether or not the act accomplished the anticipated outcomes. Remember that unlike the common perception that reason and emotion are polar opposites, Macmurray posited that emotion can be objective and placed on the same basis as reason. How the agent acts upon their feeling determines the form of the mode of reflection.

Personal relations are another form of action and can thus be framed in the cycle of withdrawal and return. According to Macmurray the fact that we are constantly withdrawing from and reestablishing relationships is vital to our development as human beings since it is by withdrawal we are able to adapt our response to another agent and reforge the relationship in a new way. In other words, we are continually learning through our relationships how to be human; even antagonistic relationships develop agency and will. All the tensions that define human existence emerge through relationships in which we either face opposition or gather support from others. Two factors—where we focus our attention and the mode of reflection we adopt—help us develop various representations of human relationships, i.e. different forms of knowledge that will inform future actions. In this case the upper portion of the cycle corresponds to a relation building phase in which the agent seeks personal connection followed by a phase of withdrawal (the bottom, reflective part of the cycle) to reflect on the interaction.

While the cycle of withdrawal and return captures the relationship between action and knowledge, there are several ways it can be misinterpreted. First, although the cycle is drawn with a Self and Other pole and by separate reflecting and acting phases, Macmurray views this process as a unity and not separable into distinct phases. In other words, it cannot be broken into component parts, taught separately, and reassembled. The only portion of the cycle that can be clearly defined in time is the moment of action. Second, although the cycle is continuous the starting point of the cycle, and thus the starting point of development, is the intent to act. Third, action can be classified into both *practical activities* that are intended to modify the Other in some way and *theoretical activities* that are intended to modify the agent's representation or knowledge of the Other. "*A practical activity is one which intends a modification of the Other; a theoretical activity is one which intends a modification in the representation of the Other.*" [42, p. 178]. Finally, the cycle is not linear in time. The duration of each step of the cycle of withdrawal and return is irrelevant. At the extreme an agent may spend his/her life devoted to the theoretical activity of science with the result that his/her actions result in knowledge that allows for greater freedom of action whether or not that action is ever performed.

In summary, the cycle of withdrawal and return describes how we continually and iteratively develop as humans. Our knowledge derives from action that begins when an agent plans an action based on a conscious and rational intention drawn from past experience which is then modified by their unconscious motive. Motive depends on the emotional valuation an agent places on the intended action, their past experience, and how often they have previously performed the action; i.e., whether it is habitual or not. The agent then acts and immediately following action pays attention to some, but not all, consequences resulting from that action. In the period of reflection following action it is what the agent pays attention to that results in building understanding of the action's result. An agent can reflect in different ways, and the way the agent reflects leads to different knowledge being created that in turn will inform future action. The repetition of this cycle over time develops habits which also serve to modify the agent's intention.

All educators have a philosophy, or set of coherent beliefs, of how students develop, whether or not they can state them explicitly. Macmurray's rhythm of withdrawal and return frames one such set of beliefs in a framework that is both broadly applicable and approachable. As one element of a coherent philosophy of engineering education the cycle of withdrawal and return offers several advantages. One is that the rhythm of withdrawal and return parallels the pragmatic, iterative, and contextualized ways that engineers arrive at design solutions. Second the balance between theory and practice is often contested in engineering degree programs and by integrating both it may lead to more productive dialogs. The cycle also highlights that learning occurs continuously and socially, not just in formal learning environments or instructor mandated assignments. In the framework of the rest of this exploration, the cycle of withdrawal and return is used to anchor further discussions of how students develop into persons.

4

WE CAN ONLY KNOW WHAT WE CAN PERCEIVE – MODES OF APPERCEPTION

"You can't be human if you live by statistics."

Macmurray, *Freedom in the Modern World*, p. 215

The last chapter introduced Macmurray's rhythm of withdrawal and return that describes how engineering students, or any person, develop through a cycle of action and reflection. While all persons learn through undergoing the action and reflection cycle, differences in perspective between agents arise in part from the modes of reflection they adopt; this is shown by the three lines branching from the reflection stage of Figure 3.1. Reflection determines what we pay attention to, how we interpret the results of our actions, and our intention for future actions. Following Descartes and Kant, Macmurray uses the term *mode of apperception* to describe how our view of the world and other persons is constructed through reflection. The term apperception—*ap* (towards) + *perception* (sense)—refers to the process of how sensory input or perceptions interface with mental constructs in ways that allow an interpretation based on context and past experience. The term apperception is historical [77, ch. 14] and not in common use today, having been replaced with more specific terminology such as selective attention in psychology or the broadly defined term mindset in education. Unlike sensation, which is the raw information from the senses that a person cannot consciously control, apperception is deliberate, and we are able to adopt different modes of apperception.

Referring back to Figure 3.1, actions are based on what the agent intends to accomplish modified by their subconscious motive, with the results of the action determined by the skill they have. As the agent moves to the reflective phase the mode of apperception they adopt determines which of the many possible results of their action they will pay attention to, what meanings they draw from the results of their action, and how the sense they make from the results integrates with existing knowledge and schemas. It is in this way that the mode of reflection determines our internal reality and affects the plans for, and results of, future actions. The three modes of apperception in Figure 3.1—generalization, particularization, and personalization—are thus central in determining how education (or any agentic action) shapes a person and indirectly the community and society they belong to.

An individual is not defined by one of these modes, rather each mode is present to various degrees in all of us and each mode serves to support a different form of learning from the results of action. However, for the agent to act effectively in a way that is both satisfactory and moral they need to engage all three modes. The degree to which each mode is expressed within an individual, however, depends on their history of past actions since repetition and habituation are key factors in developing modes of apperception. In other words, as the agent develops over time some modes can become habitual and while others require conscious mental effort; this in turn can determine or limit our capacity for action. Modes of apperception can thus be thought of as habits of attention and response that are developed over time and once established can be difficult to break out of.

The cycle of withdrawal from and return to action develops modes of apperception—i.e., ways of reflecting or mindsets—within an agent. While all a person's actions and interactions develop these modes, they are also developed explicitly within educational institutions. Thus the form of a curriculum helps to determine the actions a student takes, what they learn from their actions, and how those actions affect others. In engineering education, the form of the curriculum and assessment will contribute to students' modes of apperception which in turn serve to define, and over time determine, the bounds and values of the profession. In his Gifford Lectures Macmurray introduced three modes of apperception that align with different ways of perceiving and understanding the

world in which the agent acts.   Each of the three modes of
apperception is introduced below then discussed in the context of
the action-reflection cycle of Figure 3.1.   Each of the three modes,
and a fourth mode relevant for engineers, will be developed in more
depth in the context of engineering education in subsequent
chapters.

Generalization –
the intellectual or pragmatic mode

The intellectual/pragmatic mode of apperception occurs when the
agent's attention is focused on ways to build a representation that
can better inform subsequent action.   Following an action, the agent
uses their intellect and reason to draw broad conclusions from the
results of their action that enables them to make future action more
effective.   The pragmatic mode generalizes the results from an action
to create knowledge that supports subsequent action, and thus sees
the agent's world or environment as a means to future action.   An
example of the pragmatic mode in engineering education is the
expectation that by doing assigned homework problems students
will learn from their mistakes to become proficient at solving future
examples of the same class of problems.   Because the agent focuses
on the result of their own actions to improve their own future
efficacy, the pragmatic mode is not heterocentric and is classified by
Macmurray as negative, which in his terminology means not
concerned with the welfare of other persons.   In a discussion of ends
and means, the pragmatic mode of apperception focuses on the most
effective means to accomplish a desired future action.   In the
example given above it could be, and often is, argued that more
skillful engineers do indirectly benefit others.   While indirect
benefits can accrue, in terms of the cycle of Figure 3.1, the main focus
of reflection is on the agent themselves.

Macmurray identifies pure science as the archetype of the pragmatic
mode of apperception since in the stereotypical view of an absent-
minded scientist they are focused solely on refining their own

representations, perhaps through experiment (a form of action). Macmurray, who wrote before Kuhn [2], notes that in choosing what to investigate scientists are swayed by emotions, but most often frame science as a purely rational and disinterested pursuit. Science seen in this way thus represents pure means as does engineering if it is viewed in a purely technical sense as the application of science. In part due to the continued emphasis of engineering science in engineering degree programs [23], [62] the way engineering is mostly taught in educational institutions today predominately aligns with the pragmatic mode of apperception. Such focus is evidenced, as will be discussed further in chapter seven, by observing that most engineering curricula focus on having students practice solving engineering problems so they will become proficient at solving more challenging problems in the future.

Particularization –
the emotional, or contemplative mode

Although rational reflection is highly effective at informing how to better perform subsequent actions it can only inform whether the action is effective; emotional valuation of the act is needed to determine if it will be significant or meaningful to the agent. If, in the moment of pause following action, the agent emotionally gauges the satisfaction they feel on completion of an act then the contemplative mode of apperception is engaged. The representation of the action created by an agent in the emotional/contemplative mode seeks to be accurate in all particulars and allow emotional valuation of the act for its own sake. By capturing the Other in an emotional context that is drawn from particulars of the action the agent engages in art rather than science. Compared to generalization, which captures whether an action was effective or not, particularization determines whether the action was emotionally satisfactory to the agent. The singular focus of attention developed in the contemplative mode also allows the agent to better judge the nature of the Other. In Macmurray's system the contemplative mode is also classified as a negative since it is inward rather than outward looking and focuses on the impact of our action on our own emotional state. In a discussion of ends and means, the contemplative mode of apperception enables the agent to determine the most satisfactory end that can be achieved through their actions.

While both the pragmatic and contemplative modes coexist within the agent there are key differences between them. First, it is possible to go from the contemplative mode to the pragmatic mode (i.e., generalize from particulars) but the agent cannot with any accuracy go the other way; emotions can become rational observations, but reason cannot accurately create emotion after the fact. Second, it is not reasonable to claim that rational modes are objective while emotional modes are subjective since both originate within the mind of the agent. In other words, humans both feel and think, and both our feelings and thoughts originate within us (based on the cycle shown in Figure 3.1) so that at some level the objective and subjective are inseparable. Finally, since both modes of reflection coexist, it is not reasonable to value one over the other unless the agent is willing to commit herself to action based on this valuation. One of the goals Macmurray sought to achieve through his system was to remove the artificial duality inherent to Cartesian rationalism by better connecting emotions and intellect. The cycle of withdrawal and return defines our development as a person, and a person is a unity, even if one mode of reflection may be dominant in some situations. Macmurray holds that the exclusive reliance upon the rational mode has held back Western philosophy from being able to inform action in the world to achieve a greater good.

While the contemplative mode at first glance seems distant to engineering education, a recurring topic in STEM education is the need for the inclusion of art, STEAM, and the humanities, SHTEAM. The need for art in STEM is generally discussed in a utilitarian framework, to improve students' creativity [63]. From Macmurray's perspective, however, discussions of STEAM that adopt a pragmatic framework miss the mark since art is related to a different, but equally necessary, way of seeing the world, or developing modes of apperception, than engineering does. From the perspective of

Macmurray's system the need for art in engineering education is to develop the capacity to value one's experiences and find meaning and satisfaction in them as will be discussed in a subsequent chapter.

Personalization –
the personal or moral mode

Where the pragmatic mode of reflection generalizes rules for future action and the contemplative mode captures the satisfactoriness of an action in detail, the personal mode is concerned with how our actions affect others. While the pragmatic and contemplative modes of reflection enable the agent to act effectively and for significant ends, they do not by themselves determine whether an agent's action contributes to good. In Macmurray's system the basic unit of humanity is not "I" but "Us", and all actions are performed on a field of other agents to whom we are deeply connected; mutual dependence is the central fact of personal existence. We co-construct realities with others, and without them these realities collapse or as Macmurray frames it, *"we need each other to be ourselves."* What is good for one agent may be harmful to another, and it is the personal mode of apperception that enables the agent to perceive such effects and act morally to align means to ends. By using the personal mode an agent views their actions through the lens of their effect on others, so the personal mode of apperception is classified as positive since it is fundamentally heterocentric. Although each of the three modes of apperception—pragmatic, contemplative, and personal— contribute to rational reflection, Macmurray considers the personal mode as primary since it is the first mode we learn as humans and thus underlies all other forms of learned reflection[5].

Like the other modes, the personal mode of apperception is only defined through action in the cycle of withdrawal and return where it is developed through caring for others' welfare and freedom and by paying attention to these aspects of our actions. In Macmurray's framework morality cannot be determined independently from relational action with others since we cannot develop the personal mode of reflection without engaging in relationships. Just as there are educational challenges in learning to think procedurally to accomplish some task or in developing aesthetic contemplation, Macmurray holds a similar effort is needed to learn to develop personal relations. Developing the personal mode of apperception requires we engage in relationships and do so from a motive of love by holding the intention that our actions are for others' benefit. The love – fear duality in Macmurray's system plays a large role in the personal mode because it is challenging to develop positive relations with others when our interactions are based on fear. An additional challenge in developing the personal mode of apperception is the fact that we tend to depersonalize others as we extend our relationships since it becomes difficult to retain the notion of persons for those we will never meet or only interact with casually. According to Macmurray developing this mode of apperception requires being willing to try to personalize all relationships by caring for others rather than ourselves, recognizing the importance of others' individuality and agency, recognizing that each of us is realized through others, and treating relations with others as an end in themselves rather than as a means to an end. It is this struggle, to see all others as persons and act accordingly, that for Macmurray defines what it is to be human.

For Macmurray the personal mode of apperception addresses the dualism between knowing and acting, that knowledge requires certainty, but action requires freedom. In other words, for knowledge to be complete the future must be determinate, but freedom—the ability to act to change the future with intention— requires an indeterminate future. The role of the personal mode of apperception in society is to identify a "middle path" that accepts uncertainty and integrates reflection with action, or one's inner life with an external life in society. Knowledge and action are always in dynamic relationship with the outcome determined both by reflection and intention. Navigating this dualism is extremely difficult and it is never an easy task to act in the right way towards others. The personal mode of apperception cannot be developed without engaging in relationships or without risk to oneself. The freedom to act always implies that actions affect both the agent and the community of which the agent is a part. Macmurray equates the ability to reflect with rationality since it is only through reflection we are able to obtain the knowledge needed to act in a way aligned with our intention.

Modes of Apperception in Action

This brief introduction to the three modes of apperception illustrates why two agents who hold different modes of reflection may draw very different conclusions when they undertake the same action. The cycle of withdrawal and return is not an engineering process with fixed start and end points, but rather a continuum through which each agent is constantly moving. In this continuum the modes of apperception and the knowledge they generate define developmental pathways. Both intention and attention play a role in determining which mode is appropriate in a given situation just as which mode an agent has developed into a habit influences their intention and what they pay attention to.

If the agent's intention in acting is to improve their performance — choosing the right means to achieve their intention — then the pragmatic mode is appropriate and knowledge gained by acting serves as a means to future action. This mode addresses means only, and ultimately finds general rules that support action. If, on the other hand, the agent's intention is to arrive at an emotionally satisfying end as a result of their action they engage in the contemplative form of reflection. This mode seeks to expose form and refine sensibility in understanding the Other so that better ends can be chosen; in this sense the contemplative mode is idealistic. Conversely if the agent's intention is to develop positive relationships with another agent or community then the personal mode of apperception is appropriate. Only by acting to support the freedom of others, however, can the agent act for good.

From the perspective of attention, the pragmatic mode focuses the agent's attention on determining whether an effective and ineffective means of accomplishing an action was taken. In the contemplative mode the agent's attention focuses on determining whether the result of the action was emotionally satisfactory or unsatisfactory, i.e., determining whether the action was significant or not. Similarly in the personal mode the agent's attention is focused on building heterocentric relations with other persons that contribute to their freedom.

Because all the modes of apperception work synergistically, agents need to develop each of them if they are to be effective (pragmatic mode) in undertaking personally significant (contemplative mode) actions that do good (personal mode) in the world. The fact that the personal mode determines the effects of actions on others is why it is central in Macmurray's system. Since an agent can act skillfully and understand the nature of other agents yet still act to cause harm neither pragmatic skill nor choosing a satisfactory approach ensures an agent's actions are moral. Since neither skill nor aesthetic judgment has an inherently moral dimension, it is the extent to which an agent has developed the personal mode that determines their ability to act morally in Macmurray's framework.

In Macmurray's system the modes of apperception address two of the major changes he sought to make to mainstream Western philosophy, bringing emotional development and the relational nature of existence to the same level of consideration that rationality is held in. Macmurray's framing of modes of apperception are relevant for a philosophy of engineering education since they highlight that it is not just what we learn but how we integrate it into our actions that is important. For example, it is an interesting mental exercise to imagine the form of development that is supported as the iterative cycle of withdrawal and return (Figure 3.1) is played out over many homework and examination cycles in an engineering degree program. As will be argued in subsequent chapters, engineering education predominately adopts the pragmatic mode of apperception and thus may unintentionally limit students' ability to gain satisfaction from their work or to act for good. The pragmatic mode also does not reflect the lived practice of engineering.

Although engineering views itself as rational and pragmatic, serving as the means to clearly articulated societal needs, the reality of engineering practice is that it is a social process [64]. Without developing all modes of apperception it is difficult to succeed as an engineer given engineering's public identity as a profession dedicated to the common good and the need for self-regulation as an element of professional identity [65].

5

HOW ACTIONS AFFECT OTHERS –
THE WORLD AS ONE ACTION

"...if a particular mode of apperception is generally characteristic for any community of persons, it will determine the moral outlook which is normal in that community..."

Macmurray, *Persons in Relation*, p. 120.

The previous two chapters introduced the rhythm of withdrawal and return as a continual process through which agents develop as persons through a cycle of action and reflection and three modes of apperception in that cycle which define how agents understand and learn from the results of their acts. The third theme central to Macmurray's work is termed *the principle of the world as one action*, reflecting that our actions inevitably affect others, as their actions affect us.

There are two ways to look at the effect of our actions on others. If we adopt the position that we are isolated intellects in the Cartesian sense, then to affect others an agent must purposely and rationally choose to do so. However, Macmurray's system is relational rather than isolationist, i.e., the fundamental unit of humanity is persons in relation, so an agent's actions will always affect others whether they will it or not. As agents we can choose either to believe that our actions are mostly isolated and do not affect others unless we wish them to, or that we are continually and irrevocably connected to a larger whole. The belief system we adopt affects our intention and modes of reflection and thus affects the actions that we take and how we develop as persons. If we believe in connection then we must accept that the beliefs of other persons, our community, and society at large will affect our actions and beliefs as our actions will affect them.

Which belief system an agent chooses to adopt influences how they see both the past and the future. By adopting the Cartesian perspective, the past is viewed a collection of intentions and actions of individual agents that are effectively disconnected from each other. The course of history is determined by luck or power. Accepting the relatedness of human existence lets us understand the past through the interaction of individual agents whose collective actions result in larger societal intentions and change the course of events. If we accept that we are bound together in action, then theoretically there is one history, that of humankind, and we may be involved in a single, greater action that Macmurray refers to as *the world as one action*. Because our actions change the world, it is through the ensemble of all agents the world comes to be as it is. The principle of the world as one action as used by Macmurray explains how the action – reflection cycles and the modes of reflection that agents adopt form a constellation that dictates the form of society. Today this principle is more commonly called reflexivity.

In essence the world as one action highlights that accepting Macmurray's relational view of human existence means our actions matter not just to ourselves or those we interact with personally, but to society at large as well as those persons who do not yet exist but will in the future. Macmurray's reflexive model is in contrast to the dualistic, Cartesian model where an observer can stand apart from society to learn the truth but not have to live by that truth. From the perspective of the rhythm of withdrawal and return and modes of apperception, the principle of the world as one action extends the cycle of Figure 3.1 from a series of disconnected actions and reflections to a single, continuous, unfolding action of which the agent is but one part. This is represented (poorly) in Figure 5.1. Time flows from bottom to top and at a given moment, in the center of the diagram, an agent undertakes an action as they go through the cycle of withdrawal and return. The particular moment in time and location of the action is a single occurrence, or in engineering terminology is localized like a Dirac delta function. This particular action is informed, however, by actions from other agents which took place earlier in time. Actions immediately preceding the moment under consideration may have a direct impact (solid arrows) while earlier actions have indirect impact (dashed arrows). The further one goes back in time the larger the number of influencing actions, although their influence may get weaker. Similarly the action of the agent may influence future actions taken by other agents. As with the past, going further into the future expands the scope but weakens the direct and indirect influences. The principle of the world as one action indicates that actions inevitably affect other agents since the nature of human existence is fundamentally relational. In this model the separate actions of many agents are recorded as a continuum that together reflect mutual and societal rather than individual intentions and it is through shared intentions that individuals become bound together in a community or society. Kallenberg has described how centers of conversation in engineering design give rise to a similar evolution of ideas [19].

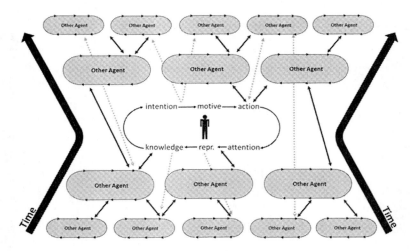

Figure 5.1: *The cycle of withdrawal and return affects other agents (person icons) whose actions in turn affect still others as outlined in the principle of the world as one action.*

At a moral or ethical level the notion of the world as one action is intriguing since it potentially provides a lens to judge our actions in the world given its similarities to Kant's categorical imperative. At the practical level, however, the notion is somewhat absurd since no individual has the wisdom or knowledge to judge the full scope of their actions in the unfolding panorama of history. While we all may be bound together in creating the world that is to be, one person cannot know what the impact of their actions will be. Seeking such knowledge veers into metaphysical questions, an area of philosophy that has generally not been held in high repute in the 20th century when logical positivism was on the rise [34], [66].

Macmurray points out, however, that this disrepute stems from the emphasis that philosophy places on "I think", i.e., rational test and verification. From the perspective of "I do" metaphysical questions can be verified through action. This same divide is found between the abstract and timeless reasoning of science and mathematics and the contingent and particular reasoning of engineering, particularly the iterative understanding developed through design and Koen's notion of heuristics [27], [48], [67]. Echoing pragmatists such as William James and John Dewey, Macmurray points out that acting as if one knew the answer to a metaphysical question has practical consequences which inform the cycle of withdrawal and return and thus impact the world. In our day-to-day lives metaphysical questions matter since we would not seek to live in a wholly rational (i.e., deterministic) world nor a world in which only the isolated mind exists since both deny the possibility of action and therefore change. In engineering education metaphysical questions matter to students who are not just struggling with what they should learn, but at a more fundamental level who they should become [68].

The reason Macmurray starts his philosophy with "I do" is that our actions matter and irrevocably bind us to others. The reality of how we actually live in the world does not reflect a philosophy based on "I think". Rather we live and act as if both our actions and their effect on others matter, even if we cannot comprehend the full extent of these effects. In acting this way, we determine a way of life that binds the world together in one action since my acts inevitably affect other agents. To act we must have some conception of the world we wish to exist and an intention to bring it about. It is for this reason that we must anticipate the ends of our actions and not merely the means by which we make changes to the world based on our intent. The questions posed early in this book about what the ends of engineering education could or should be are important because of the fact that engineers are educated to possess the means to make significant change.

In his Gifford Lectures Macmurray used the principle of the world as one action to encompass how our actions as an agent affect other agents through our relationships as well as how the modes of apperception that are dominant in society affect how we develop as persons. How we develop relations with other persons is determined by the cycle of withdrawal and return, particularly our motive and the mode of apperception we adopt. As agents continually reforge their relationships over time their unconscious motives of love or fear and whether they succeed or fail at a relationship determine the form of future relationships. The ideal case occurs when an agent acts from love and their action to build a relationship succeeds. In this case the relationship strengthens and there is mutual growth in fellowship. Another positive outcome is when the agent has a motive of love but their action fails, triggering withdrawal and reflection because the intended relationship is frustrated. If the reason their action failed was that they chose the correct action but either used the wrong means to achieve their intent or were unskilled in its application then the pragmatic mode of reflection enables the agent to develop intellectual judgment. On the other hand, if the agent realizes that they acted the wrong way because they misread the intent of the other person then the personal or contemplative modes of reflection develop moral or emotional judgment. In either case the agent is better equipped to pursue relationships in the future. If, however, the agent's motive is fear for themselves or fear of another then they will over time either seek to gain control over others through misuse of the pragmatic mode of reflection or withdraw from further relationships by retreating inward through the contemplative mode of apperception.

The mode of apperception an agent adopts also has a strong effect on the type of relationship (personal, impersonal, direct, or indirect) they build. The ideal mode of interacting is to adopt the personal mode of apperception and be attentive to creating freedom for other agents. There may be times, however, in which it is appropriate to adopt the pragmatic or contemplative mode. For example, a physician may adopt the pragmatic mode to maintain a needed objective distance from a patient that they are in direct relationship with, but switch to the personal mode when interacting with their family [59]. An artist, on the other hand, adopts a contemplative mode to capture the image of a model on canvas but later may present their work to an impersonal audience or public who in turn develop an indirect relationship with the artist's subject. In other words, the modes of apperception we adopt enable us to support different forms of relationships with others. Macmurray is clear, however, that the ability to build meaningful and beneficial relationships, and thus undertake moral actions, arises from developing the personal mode of apperception.

Since we are constantly interacting with others, which mode of reflection we adopt also affects the tone of our community and, at a larger scale, society. While in a small community it is relatively easy to maintain personal relations, it becomes more difficult to support such relations as the size of a community grows. In larger societies although individuals do have personal relationships, *indirect* and *impersonal* connections between agents predominate, and politics and economics take the place of friendships in supporting moral behavior and maintaining justice or fair relationships [69]. To maintain justice society sets up contracts and laws for the case when people do not act morally in indirect relations and the government maintains social cooperation by enforcing laws. Thus law serves as a means to the end of justice and the State serves as a proxy for community. Implied in these relations is a hierarchy of importance where moral action (freedom for persons) is at the top, justice is next as a proxy for maintaining community and freedom, law and contracts are one step lower since they are the means that support justice, and the State or other organization is at the bottom since it is in a purely pragmatic role to serve as the means to the ends of morality and justice.

Central to Macmurray's development of the principle of the world as one action is that the modes of apperception broadly adopted by individuals in a society help determine the structures [10] which affect agents' behaviors in society. The relationship is bi-directional: the most prevalent modes of personal relationships determine the form of society and societal modes of apperception affect our own development and thus how we come to view the world [70]. The principle of the world as one action thus captures how predominate modes of apperception affect societies. In his Gifford Lectures Macmurray contrasts three forms of society that align with the pragmatic, contemplative, and personal modes of apperception and adopt either the mechanistic, organic, or personal forms of morality respectively (chapter 2). These forms are important for engineering education since they determine what aims of education are valued by society which in turn influences the form of the curriculum [57] and what students learn.

Pragmatic Mode Societies: Western cultures generally adopt a pragmatic mode of apperception and view society as a State since our political systems arose from Roman societies that used the law as a tool to unite heterogeneous populations [42]. Hobbes' *Leviathan* [71] serves as the archetype of the pragmatic mode at a societal level, claiming it is rational to form a state since the State can enforce cooperation between agents. The pragmatic mode of apperception that underlies this view of a State assumes that some general set of rules, in this case law, are required to bind together a society and through this process the community becomes more efficient. In such a society law serves both to regulate morality and to maintain equilibrium in relationships. Moral behavior arises through self-control as espoused by the Stoics [46] and Kant [72]. A society based on this mode is technological and guided by efficiency. If these societies become driven by a motive of fear, however, they can focus on domination through law and thus drift towards authoritarianism. Pragmatic societies also operate on an underlying assumption that law is required since people will seek advantage. Macmurray notes that this assumption does not easily permit the better nature of people to emerge, an observation that parallels more recent critiques of the rational actor models that modern economic theories are based on [72], [73]. Societies that evolve from the pragmatic mode undervalue personal modes of existence and are predominantly "engineered" to be functional. Although not discussed by Macmurray, it would be expected that societies based on the pragmatic mode of apperception value education in engineering and the other STEM disciplines given their focus on utility.

Contemplative Mode Societies: The contemplative mode of apperception at a societal level, arising from Greek roots, is represented in more modern philosophical movements by Rousseau's *The Social Contract* [74] that assumed man in his natural state is inherently good. The goal of society is then to find the most satisfactory role for its members and the structure of such societies is based on forms and roles, e.g., Plato's *Republic* [75]. In such a world we are able to give ourselves to the process of society and through collective effort advance towards an ideal. Macmurray uses the term organic to describe societies that adopt the contemplative mode. In such societies most agents are spectators, and the actors are discouraged from deviating from their roles since this causes discord from the perceived ideal. As the contemplative mode of apperception focuses inwardly on the ideal, Rousseau's view of society mistakes what should be for what actually is. Macmurray points out that since such societies support an internal life of the mind they can be prone to control by those who set the ideals. Compared to the more mechanistic pragmatic societies, broad adoption of the contemplative mode of apperception leads to a society in which its members are expected to serve in roles that support societal functions.

Personal Mode Societies: When the personal mode of apperception, deriving from Hebrew and Christian traditions, is applied to society it focuses on whether the actions of the society are moral, i.e., enhance the freedom of all members. An example from Sedlacek's commentary on modern capitalist economic theory [72] is the Hebrew practice of Shemittah that cancelled debt every seven years.

While this practice is humane, it does not make sense from the perspective of pragmatic mode societies. The goal of a society based on the personal mode is to seek "realness" or authenticity in relationships and freedom for its members. While the pragmatic mode seeks the right means to operate efficiently and the contemplative mode seeks satisfactory ends through ideals, the personal mode seeks to integrate correct means with satisfactory ends to maximize freedom for all agents. Historically, western societies have placed the State in a position of central authority over persons' economic and political lives while religion plays the central role in defining standards of personal relationships. Ideally the role of religion is to help members of society arrive at truth about relationships, in essence expressing the conscience of a community. Religion succeeds in this role when it supports relationships based on love and fails if it is egocentric, self-serving, or grounded in fear. If the community's mode of apperception is pragmatic, then religion serves as a "spiritual technology" to control external forces that affect our lives such as suffering and loss. In contrast, a community using the contemplative mode of reflection uses religion to express utopian visions to allow members of society to look internally and withdraw from the world as it is.

Macmurray argued that dysfunctional political and economic systems arise, in part, when pragmatic or contemplative modes of apperception are overly dominate within a society. Societies that adopt the contemplative mode tend towards romanticism as people assign personal functions to, or personalize, organizations. In other words, organizations take over from humans in providing community. Personalizing an organization—be it a commercial firm or government—detracts from the freedom of persons since those who determine what the correct form of relations should be are able to force others into idealized roles[6]. In contrast in societies that predominantly utilize the pragmatic mode of apperception organizations become ends in themselves and efficiency becomes valued for its own sake. In such mechanistic societies what is right becomes what is possible and the valuation of efficiency creates a positive feedback cycle where actions are done not for the sake of community or personal freedom, but for the sake of power. Law, commerce, and technological advancement then become the definition of justice, not a means to justice, and moral actions are defined as those which align with the interests of organizations. Societies drift towards authoritarianism when political or economic power becomes an end in itself rather than a means to human thriving. One of Macmurray's goals was to counter such drift towards authoritarianism by describing how the personal mode of apperception enables a society to reflect on its actions in a way that directs attention to issues of community and freedom.

The relevance of the principle of the world as one action for engineering education arises from the fact that the modes of apperception held by those who have influence in society set the tone of that society. In Macmurray's writings he focused on how Law reflects a society's will towards and beliefs about justice. Given the role that technology plays in day-to-day life in developed countries engineers also have a large influence on society since the choice of which engineering projects to pursue reflects similar ideals of justice. Societies that adopt personal modes of reflection create laws and undertake projects that help ensure relationships are just. In societies adopting pragmatic or contemplative modes law and technology serves to protect the power or image of organizations at the expense of individuals. Furthermore, how the law or technology adapts to changes in society will be driven by the dominant mode of apperception. In pragmatic societies the technology and laws serve to maintain power structures, in contemplative societies they will maintain appearances, and in personal societies they support community and personal freedom. The modes of apperception that engineers hold and how they see their role matter greatly to the form of society.

This chapter has briefly reviewed how the principle of the world as one action frames how students' development affects relationships in, and thus the tone of, a community and society. Each of us has a choice of seeing our actions as isolated or connected. Choosing the path of connection places an obligation on both students and educators to understand how the form of a person's development helps sets the tone of society. Furthermore, because the modes of apperception valued by society are instantiated in education systems, they influence how students are educated. If engineering educators wish to achieve different or improved outcomes from education the principle of the world as one action suggests this could be accomplished through developing appropriate modes of apperception in students and helping them better understand how societal beliefs impact their education. At the level of a course or the curriculum the world as one action indicates that the development of professional skills such teamwork depends upon the effects of habits and motive developed in other courses and a student's ability to develop personal rather than merely professional relations with peers [76]. At a policy level the implications for engineering education are that educational outcomes are strongly influenced by the beliefs of individuals, suggesting a shift in focus from programs and outcomes to students. Such shifts are important because the values of society also impact engineering works since they are similarly embedded within a larger social fabric. The work of engineers has widespread societal impacts, particularly as society comes to increasingly rely on technology for basic human needs. The fact that engineering responds to human needs, and all engineering work takes place within larger social, economic, technological, and environmental systems highlights that the beliefs and practices of engineers affect society. In other words, because the work of engineering educators matters greatly it is incumbent on engineering education to provide students understanding of their own development as persons and their choices impact the larger systems to which they are connected.

6

THE SYSTEMIC MODE OF APPERCEPTION

"Fear not; the things that you are afraid of are quite likely going to happen to you, but they are nothing to be afraid of."

MacMurray, *Persons in Relation*, p. 171

The previous chapters outlined the philosophical system John Macmurray published in The Self as Agent [40] and Persons in Relation [41]. This system puts action before knowledge to address a divide between practical and theoretical views of the world which Macmurray believed made Western society value intellectual over emotional and personal development. Macmurray's system describes how persons develop through a cycle of action and reflection by adopting three synergistic modes of reflection: pragmatic/intellectual, contemplative/emotional, and personal/moral. Macmurray's system serves as a good starting point for exploring the role of philosophy in engineering education since the focus on action in his system aligns with the contingent reasoning of engineering [48] and its iterative and developmental aspects aligns with current views of education. Since all action is relational, a student must develop knowledge of other agents with whom the student is engaged in action which captures the broad discussion of professional skills in engineering education. Macmurray's system also explicitly places the person in a central position, thereby defining good as enabling other individuals to develop fully as persons and building and maintaining a community that allows such development. This definition aligns with espoused value systems in both education and engineering which prioritize human welfare [65].

This chapter expands on Macmurray's system to develop an additional mode of apperception for the cycle of withdrawal and return of Figure 3.1 that is asserted to be relevant for engineering students. Macmurray saw his philosophy as a framework for others to expand upon, and prior work had explored elements of his system in education [38]. To satisfy the criteria of uniqueness any new mode should enable an agent to develop intentions different than those suggested by the three existing modes as well as shift their attention in ways that allows them to see new consequences of their actions. Because modes of apperception have a moral element, it should inform right actions. Additionally any engineering-specific mode of apperception should align with how engineering is defined in use as a human activity [27], [77], how engineering educators define relevant content domains [78], and what engineers actually do in their roles [64], [79].

To develop a mode of apperception relevant to the many disciplines within engineering it is worthwhile to understand how engineering defines itself. Today's definitions of engineering do not differ that much from that found in Thomas Tredgold's 1828 charter founding the Institution of Civil Engineers which defines engineering as *"...the art of directing the great sources of power in Nature for the use and convenience of man"*. There have been many modifications to this basic definition, for example the Accreditation Board for Engineering and Technology's (ABET) definition of engineering design [80], but the general idea of modification of nature for human benefit are retained. Koen [27], Bucciarelli [64], and Cross [81] see the process of modification, i.e., design, as central to engineering, particularly iterative design driven by heuristics and design practiced in a social context. While design is practiced widely outside engineering, it is central to engineering epistemology and this serves as the basis for developing a new mode of apperception. Unlike science, which seeks universals, the fact that design is embedded in changing and uncertain human needs and must manage multiple constraints gives engineering knowledge a more contingent nature [23] than that of science. Implicit to engineering practice, particularly design, is the assumption that engineers have developed senses or means to perceive the world (natural, technological, social, economic, etc.) in ways that allow them to intend actions that modify it in a way beneficial to their clients or employers. The ability to sense and make judgements based on what they perceive implies a mode of apperception that allows them to interpret the results of actions in a way they can modify intentions and future actions. Furthermore, if the modification is to be done in a beneficial way the mode of apperception has to draw on some coherent system of morality, which for engineers is framed as codes of ethics.

As discussed previously with the example of a jet engine, engineers' perceptions are drawn from both their own senses and technology that extends those senses. The information that is measured or perceived is used heuristically by comparing the data to a model or representation of the system that the engineer seeks to build or modify. While all people to a greater or lesser extent create constructs to test actions against [82], the activity of iteratively refining models or representations that guide action is a central aspect of learning and practicing engineering. In particular engineers represent information in a way which enables them to manage large and complicated design projects. Key to the engineering method as it has been practiced are methods to simplify the complex nature of many projects [83].

Investigations of how engineers think during design activities find, in a broad sense, two different modes of reflection. Engineers typically use Macmurray's pragmatic mode of reflection when they are focused on achieving a design goal. This mode of design is often called convergent since the engineer heuristically and iteratively improves the design to achieve defined specifications under given constraints. The other mode is one in which the engineer broadens their perspective to understand the larger context in which the design is embedded, undertakes search strategies or problem framing to see whether the evolution of the design has identified a better pathway to a solution, and reassesses their knowledge in light of new information. This is called the divergent mode of design, and engineers often oscillate between divergent and convergent modes when doing design [67], [81]. In the divergent mode engineers look outwards to understand the larger system in which the design is embedded. Given the fact that technology (defined broadly) is ubiquitous, this system is in essence the world and society, although practically it is often viewed through a pragmatic lens based on the context, constraints, and the client of the project. As a result, engineers in the divergent phase of design ideally look at economic, environment, safety, technological, and many other factors which impinge upon the design. Studies which compare novice to expert designers show that experts tend to start in more divergent and exploratory modes of design before converging to specific solutions [84] while novices focus more on convergent modes.

Here it is proposed that the ability to see engineering work in the larger context used in the divergent phase of design corresponds to a separate mode of apperception relevant for engineering education. As mentioned previously, apperception as originally used by Kant is the capacity for awareness of a state; that is how an individual's perception through judgement creates meaning for the individual. In the case of engineering during the convergent phases of design engineers make pragmatic judgements in a manner similar to how scientists refine hypotheses. In the divergent modes of design, however, engineers seek to frame their work in a larger system and balance many, often competing, factors. As Kallenberg [19] points out, there are nearly limitless number of such factors that can be thought of as "centers of conversation" around which designs are negotiated in a social process [64]. Basset and Krupczak [85] describe the process by which universal principles are interpreted for highly contingent design activities as a reversal of the vector of abstraction. Modes of apperception have both perceptual and moral characteristics, and the ability to draw on experience and perceive how a design interacts with the larger world require both. In becoming effective designers engineering students are expected to develop the ability to perceive the larger system in which their work is embedded. However if the design work is to contribute to moral good and be beneficial, they also need to perceive how design impacts on the larger system and act to change designs which do not contribute to agency, freedom, and community. Work showing that expert designers are better able to organize and conceptualize design broadly provides some evidence that elements of a systemic mode of apperception is developed through engineering work [84]. From the perspective of Macmurray's philosophy it follows that such a mode would be developed through going through the cycle of withdrawal and return while utilizing this mode of apperception.

A systemic mode of apperception also adds to Macmurray's principle of the world as one action (chapter five). Since we are defined by action rather than thought our actions contribute to making the world as it is; by acting in the world it becomes a relational part of us. Because we are agents, however, we have a choice in how to act. We may act as if we are independent of the world or we may act as we are a part of the world and our actions help determine its future. In either case our actions will contribute to the state of the world but how we act will likely be different [40, p. 220]:

> "We exist only as agents; and in our existence we are parts of the world, dependent upon it for the support and the resistance which make our action possible. The thought of the world as a unity is a postulate of action. For any action in the world depends on the cooperation of the world. It is indeed an integration of the movements of the Agent with the movements of the Other, so that in action the Self and the Other form a unity. This integration is the action and its unity is intentional."

In other words, an engineer's ability to act in ways harmonious to the world arises from believing she is a part of the world and her fate is tied to that of others and the larger world. However, to act as if she is part of the world she must develop a mode of apperception that helps her filter her knowledge of the world in a way that informs intention, focuses attention, and which accurately lets her perceive her role in the larger system. Macmurray argues that the choice of how to act in the world—independently or as part of the larger whole—can only be determined through taking action in the world in a way that develops modes of apperception.

This remainder of this chapter broadly discusses aspects of a systemic mode of apperception that arises out of activities conducted by engineers and aligns with the philosophical framework outlined by Macmurray. This mode of apperception is relevant for engineers since over the last decades there has been increasing recognition of a broad range of issues related to how humans are modifying planetary systems. The extent of these modifications has led to the modern age being called the Anthropocene or the Great Acceleration [86]. Mitcham argues that engineering has had a central role in these changes [16]:

> "What Percy Bysshe Shelley said about poets two centuries ago applies even more to engineers today: They are the unacknowledged legislators of the world. By designing and constructing new structures, processes, and products, they are influencing how we live as much as any laws enacted by politicians."

Our ability to attribute changes in natural and human environments to human activity is due to the fact that human understanding of complex systems such as ecologies has significantly advanced since Macmurray's time. The activities of engineers have measurably changed the world and we are building increasingly accurate understanding of the effects these changes have on social and environmental systems.

To better define the systemic mode of apperception and clarify how it differs from Macmurray's pragmatic mode it is worth looking to the related areas of systems engineering and systems thinking. The term "systemic" arises from "system" which has the Greek root *systema* meaning an organized whole compounded of parts. The idea of a system arose in pre-Socratic philosophy [83] and was further framed teleologically by Aristotle. While teleology was not carried forwards in the scientific revolution, which preferred logical and causal chains of inference that broke down problems into simple elements, its ideas remained active in biology as life was difficult to break down using Descartes' principles from *A Discourse on the Method* [47]. Today's definitions of a system retain the sense of wholeness and parts but vary in details.

While systems engineering has potential to inform this mode, it retains the pragmatic focus of engineering which is practiced for specific purposes with success determined by achieving that purpose within constraints. Systems engineering, as a sub-discipline within engineering, came to prominence in the decades following the Second World War as organizations, operations, and supply chains became larger, more complex, and difficult to manage [87]. Within this discipline a system is defined as "...*an integrated composite of people, products, and processes that provide a capability to satisfy a stated need or objective.*" [88]. Similarly, systems engineering defines itself as "...*an interdisciplinary approach and a means to enable the realization of successful systems. It focuses on defining customer needs and required functionality early in the development cycle, documenting requirements, then proceeding with design synthesis and system validation while considering the complete problem.*" [89]. These definitions predominantly align with the pragmatic mode of apperception since systems are seen as needing to be managed to serve customer or other needs.

A more appropriate definition of a system for developing a mode of apperception comes from system science which arose as a synthetic and interdisciplinary field from organismal biology. Advances in computational methods of solving differential equations in the 1960's saw increased rigor and activity focused first around cybernetics and later biology [83]. The ideas of system science, such as open and closed systems, have been generalized to organizational [10], [90] and social [91] systems where it is more generally known as systems thinking. Systems thinking is a field that seeks to provide insights on how connections and interdependencies lead to behaviors which are complex and unexplainable from the models of more positivistic and linear science. In the systems thinking tradition parts of a system work to produce a greater whole leading to the definition of a system as "*...a set of things interconnected in such a way that they produce their own pattern of behavior over time.*" [31, p. 4] which goes back to Aristotle's teleology commonly expressed as "*The whole is more than the sum of its parts*"[7]. Systems thinking differs from systems engineering in that pragmatic intentions to predict and control a system by managing its interactions are viewed as futile or ineffective. Rather the view that the world is highly interconnected leads to metaphors of nurturing systems and working within, rather than managing, their functionings. These ideas are framed eloquently by Donella Meadows in Dancing with Systems [32]:

> "The goal of foreseeing the future exactly and preparing for it perfectly is unrealizable. The idea of making a complex system do just what you want it to do can be achieved only temporarily, at best. We can never fully understand our world, not in the way our reductionistic science has led us to expect. Our science itself, from quantum theory to the mathematics of chaos, leads us into irreducible uncertainty. For any objective other than the most trivial, we can't optimize; we don't even know what to optimize. We can't keep track of everything. We can't find a proper, sustainable relationship to nature, each other, or the institutions we create, if we try to do it from the role of omniscient conqueror. ... Systems thinking leads to another conclusion–however, waiting, shining, obvious as soon as we stop being blinded by the illusion of control. It says that there is plenty to do, of a different sort of "doing." The future can't be predicted, but it can be envisioned and brought lovingly into being. Systems can't be controlled, but they can be designed and redesigned. We can't surge forward with certainty into a world of no surprises, but we can expect surprises and learn from them and even profit from them. We can't impose our will upon a system. We can listen to what the system tells us, and discover how its properties and our values can work together to bring forth something much better than could ever be produced by our will alone."

Meadow's description highlights a way of seeing the world, a mental framework, that is adopted here to describe the systemic mode of apperception. Unlike the pragmatic mode that seeks to generalize the outcomes of action to improve future actions, the systemic mode provides a counterbalance to human manipulation by recognizing that all engineering work occurs within larger systems which cannot always be controlled, optimized, or even quantified. System thinking provides a lens that enables an agent to shift their intention for future actions as well as what they pay attention to following their action towards the larger impacts of their work. In this regard it meets some criteria for a mode of apperception since it enables the agent to reinterpret possible consequences of their actions.

The systemic mode of apperception also aligns well with the practice of engineering since systems thinking draws many of its ideas and methods from engineering. These include the use of mathematical models, creating diagrammatic representations to map systems, as well as a heuristic-driven process for engaging with systems productively. Mapping systems is important because their behaviors are often opaque, nonlinear, and have significant lags. Representational maps allow the circular reinforcing and damping behaviors of systems to be understood using techniques analogous to those used in engineering [91]. Many of the heuristics of systems thinking are also shared with engineering including the importance of positive and negative feedback loops, reservoirs that can lead to a lag in response times, and self-organizing behaviors. Others—such as controlling information flows, the roles of incentives, and the impact of shifting goals—are less familiar to engineers but well known by organizational or social scientists [34, ch. 6]. Within engineering design, elements of systems thinking arise in a methodology known as human-centered design. Human-centered design became popular around the 1980's and stemmed from the Scandinavian method of participatory design in the 1960's and the development of systems ergonomics in the 1950's which in turn reflected a tradition that can be traced back to Plato [92]. Human centered design seeks to understand how humans are affected systemically by a design, putting the user foremost in design decisions. To see how design affects human organizations it hypothesizes porous or flexible boundaries between human and technical systems and views technology as contributing to the human environment.

Framing the systemic mode of apperception as drawing from systems thinking and clarifying its relation to engineering as a counter-point to the pragmatic mode common in engineering enables the new mode to align with the cycle of withdrawal and return in Macmurray's system. Macmurray, drawing from Hegelian dialectics, characterized modes of apperception as positive (personal) or negative (pragmatic and contemplative) based on whether they are inward or outward facing and how they support freedom and friendship. Given that the systemic mode focuses on seeing oneself in relation to a larger system and provides insights on how to interact with rather than manipulate one's environment, the systemic mode of apperception is outward facing.

Modes of apperception as used in the cycle of withdrawal and return are more than intellectual frameworks for understanding the world. They imply that an agent's perception is steered in particular directions which affects future actions in the world, and for this reason a mode of apperception impacts on the behaviors and moral capacity of an agent. In this regard the systemic mode of apperception can be seen, similar to the personal mode of apperception, as determining the form of relationship an agent has with the Other. As defined here the relationship is positive, which in Macmurray's terminology indicates care for and friendship with what the agent acts in concert with and so care and empathy for the larger system in which the agent exists is implied in the systemic mode of apperception. Acting in this mode an engineer would view the preservation of larger systems as an end in itself rather than act from the desire to use to the system as a means, which would align with the pragmatic mode of apperception.

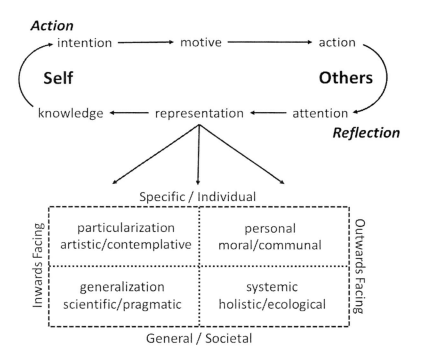

Figure 6.1: *Addition of the systemic mode of apperception to Macmurray's cycle of withdrawal and return.*

Adding the systemic mode of apperception to the cycle of withdrawal and return leads to four separate forms of representation which modify the cycle of withdrawal and return as shown in Figure 6.1. These four modes—contemplative, pragmatic, personal, and systemic—can be arranged on axes of being inwards or outwards facing (in Macmurray's terminology positive or negative) and general – specific or individual – societal. The systemic mode of apperception like the personal mode is outwards facing and values the larger systems in which engineering work is done as an end in itself. Its focus extends beyond personal relationships to consider environmental, economic, and social systems which either enable or inhibit personal relationships. The systemic mode shares the focus on generalizations with the pragmatic mode, meaning it seeks broad understanding that can inform future action. Unlike the pragmatic mode, however, it focuses on outward-facing relationships rather than action for its own sake. Broadly speaking the systemic mode enables the agent to consider the systemic effects of their actions against the Other and what effects those actions will have to change the nature of the system in which all agents are embedded. It thus has an ends- rather than the purely means-focus of the pragmatic mode.

As discussed previously, proposing a systemic mode of apperception was undertaken to better align Macmurray's system to engineering education. While the education of engineers does not generally mandate training in the social sciences, the reality is that engineered technologies affect personal relations, mostly indirectly. For example, social media is defining new forms of relationships [93] while the automobile and mass transportation fundamentally changed the characteristics of neighborhoods and the relations of individuals within them; advances in self driving vehicles will likely do so again. Similarly, engineering actions can have widespread ecological implications which can be addressed through the systemic mode. While introducing the systemic mode does not materially affect Macmurray's conceptions of justice, law, or economy as described in chapter five, it does emphasize the need to develop ways for engineering students to understand how the systemic effects of technologies may impact individual freedoms and planetary systems. The systemic mode of apperception additionally provides a lens to address one of the questions left open by Macmurray's work: determining when a community becomes a society and relations stop being personal. If the impact of actions on others makes more sense viewed from the systemic rather than the personal mode of apperception then a community has grown that it is better described as a society.

In summary, this chapter introduces a systemic mode of apperception to better align Macmurray's philosophy to engineering education. This addition expands upon the conception of the world as one action by highlighting systemic interconnections within the socio-technical-natural environment that affect persons and communities. A key characteristic of this mode of apperception is that systems are not manageable or controllable but rather need to be sensed, probed, and interacted with in a holistic partnership rather than through top-down control. While the systemic mode of apperception does not directly address friendship or the relation of persons, it is classified as positive in Macmurray's framework since it enables engineers to relate to the larger societal, economic, and environmental factors which contribute to love (or fear) and thus enable (or prevent) friendships from thriving. It will be argued in the next chapter that engineers are trained to work predominantly with pragmatic modes of apperception and focus on factors that are immediately relevant to the problem at hand with the result that the concerns of persons may be overlooked.

7
A CRITIQUE OF
ENGINEERING EDUCATION

"Here is the greatest threat to education in our own society. We are becoming more and more technically minded: gradually we are falling victims to the illusion that all problems can be solved by proper organization: that if we fail it is because we are doing the job in the wrong way, and that all that is needed is the 'know-how'. To think thus in education is to pervert education. It is not an engineering job. It is personal and human."

Macmurray, *Learning to be Human*

The introduction to this book posed several questions about engineering education in the post-modern world: What ends does engineering education claim to serve as a means to? In what ways does engineering education contribute to or hinder moral good? These questions imply that engineering education as it is currently conceived and practiced does not sufficiently define the ends toward which it works [16] and through this lapse graduates may not be prepared to identify or work towards moral ends. This chapter uses Macmurray's nascent philosophical system—particularly the rhythm of withdrawal and return, modes of apperception, the idea of the world as one action, and moral good as enabling freedom for persons—as a framework to critique the practice of engineering education.

The word critique comes from the same Greek root, *techne*, as technology but while technology is a discourse on arts, critique derives from critical arts so to critique something is not just to criticize, but to provide a detailed and critical analysis. In modern times Foucault expanded the notion of critique to implicitly include addressing the accepted knowledges and power structures which are embedded in societal structures. Habermas, echoing Macmurray in some ways, frames critique through a lens of discourse to try to establish grounds for moral norms or intersubjective validity [94]. While Foucault's and Habermas' points of view are not necessarily compatible [95] both power structures and discourse provide useful lenses for critiques.

As critique can be defined different ways, so too it is difficult to define engineering education since it covers a vast swath of knowledge from mathematics, the physical and social sciences, education, and the learning sciences as well as multiple established engineering disciplines with their own traditions and cultures. Attempts to understand the bounds of research in engineering education [96], [97] find its scope quite broad. Additionally, what engineering education is depends on who you ask; a student's conception may very different than a faculty member's which in turn is different than the CEO of a technology company faced with hiring challenges.

From the perspective of Macmurray's system, however, a perfect definition of critique or engineering education is not needed, but rather sufficient knowledge to act. A starting point is sufficient since going through the cycle of withdrawal and return, like iterative processes in engineering design, will refine our understanding and heuristics or as Koen might say push forward the state of the art [27]. Macmurray's system serves as an adequate framework for a critique since it offers a generalizable model of human development and learning, defines good in ways that align with both engineering and education, and connects individuals to the communities and societies in which they exist.

This chapter critiques engineering education from four different perspectives corresponding to the four modes of apperception discussed earlier—pragmatic, contemplative, personal, and systemic. Given that the pragmatic mode of apperception focuses on improving performance this lens is used to explore how philosophy can be practically utilized to improve the education of engineers. Similarly, the contemplative lens explores the extent to which engineering education prepares students to address issues of personal significance; the personal lens focuses on the role relationships and community have in developing as an engineer or engineering educator; and the systemic lens explores how engineering education relates to the larger systems in which its work is embedded. All four perspectives maintain a focus on action, which is what Macmurray's system suggests on ways to define the ends of engineering education and better align means with those ends. Just as the first phases of design explore the scope of a project, the goal of this chapter is to undertake a broad overview of engineering education using an exploratory and divergent approach. The next chapter will shift to the convergent mode of design to synthesize and draw conclusions from this exploration.

The Pragmatic Mode of Apperception – Engineering Education as Means

In Macmurray's pragmatic mode of apperception an agent reflects on her action in order to improve her future actions. Given that engineering is a pragmatic discipline which seeks to improve its own practices and advance the state of the art [27] this mode is arguably predominant in engineering education. The fact that engineers and engineering educators must continually adapt their practice as engineering and education change in response to societal needs leads to a pragmatic outlook where practices are continually redefined [98]. The influence of engineering ways of knowing and doing are reflected in engineering education through a focus on quality improvement and outcome evaluation. Similarly, the view of engineering education held by policy makers is based on beliefs in its utility so that policy reports typically frame the benefits of engineering, and thus the need to educate engineers, in terms of the economy, society, and national security. In short, engineering's value system has permeated much of the practice of engineering education, and engineering educators most often frame their work in pragmatic language. From this pragmatic perspective the value of philosophy, in this case Macmurray's system, arises from any insights it can offer to improve the practice of engineering education.

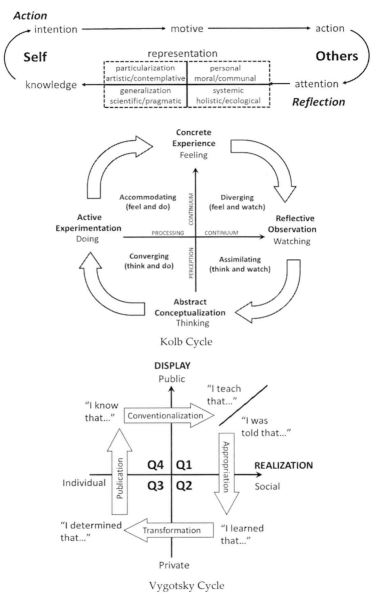

Figure 7.1: *Revised cycle of withdrawal and return (top) compared with Kolb's experiential learning cycle (bottom left) and Rom Harré's socioconstructivist Vygotsky Cycle (bottom right).*

One such insight is to provide a new perspective on how students develop the knowledge, skills, and attitudes of engineers through the cycle of withdrawal and return. The cycle of withdrawal and return of Figure 6.1 is recreated at the top of Figure 7.1 and this representation is reminiscent of several other cyclical learning models such as the Kolb cycle [99] of experiential learning or Rom Harre's socio-constructivist Vygotsky cycle [100] shown in the bottom panels of Figure 7.1. The Kolb cycle hypothesizes learning occurs in a four-stage cycle where a new experience stimulates reflection which then develops into an abstract conception which is tested through action or experimentation which creates a new experience and begins the cycle anew. Kolb also hypothesized students have different learning styles based on whether they preferred acting or observing and whether they were more prone to thinking or feeling. Kolb's learning cycle has been adapted to engineering by Cowan [101]. Rom Harre, building on Vygotsky, hypothesized students learn through a process of social construction of knowledge by internalizing what is learned, creating a personally meaningful representation, then shared their knowledge publicly to test whether the personal representation aligns with conventions.

Both of these theories have similarities with Macmurray's cycle of withdrawal and return in that some action, either individual or social, stimulates reflection which results in learning. There are, however, several key differences. One is the emphasis Macmurray places on attention since how we act in the future depends upon the focus of agent's attention following an action which influences how representations are developed and thus what actions will be valued in the future. In a very real sense where the student puts their attention determines their future. The observation that attention is focused by motive goes back to at least William James [102] and in learning attention plays a key role in consciously modifying behavior, i.e., shifting from habitual responses [103]. Unlike Kolb or Harre, Macmurray emphasizes the role played by the different modes of reflection and how these result in different habits based on a student's intention and attention. Attention, for example, matters in engineering education since while expert designers consider multiple scenarios before making design decisions students (novices) typically focus their attention, limiting the design space [104].

In designing educational interventions it may be worth building in moments which allow conscious shifting of attention in order to develop different modes of apperception. If, for example, students' attention is drawn to a mistake with the intent of making corrections to improve future performance the pragmatic mode is developed. However if attention is drawn to the emotional impact of mistakes with guidance that such emotional challenges lead to growth [105] or to a faculty mentor sharing stories of past errors in order to build a relationship then the contemplative or personal modes are developed respectively. Although most formal feedback mechanisms in engineering education develop the pragmatic mode of apperception, Macmurray is clear that to develop as a person all modes need to be engaged. If an agent's actions are to be right (moral) as well as correct (successful), navigating the action – reflection turning point of the top part of Figure 7.1 requires that beyond rational analysis of the result of their action the agent learns to correctly judge their emotional reaction, anticipate whether the action contributes to friendship and community, as well as work to understand the systemic impact of their action.

Another difference between the cycle of withdrawal and return and other cyclical models of learning is the role emotion plays. In the rhythm of withdrawal and return both conscious intention, the goal of the agent, and their conscious or unconscious motive determine action. Intention is intellectual while motive arises from emotion. As outlined in *Persons in Relation*, intentional action develops motives based on either love or fear that over time define an individual's character: "...*the persistent system of motives from which he acts under normal conditions*" [41, p. 198]. While character determines the general vector of behavior, motive can be modified by intention. Macmurray's system implies that the result of an action taken from a motive of fear will nudge students in developmental directions which intensify that fear while positive motive shifts the student towards love. Work in engineering education based on self-determination theory [106] broadly supports this observation [107]–[109]. Put simply, when learning activities are not aligned with a student's intention negative educational outcomes are more likely while alignment with intention leads to more positive intellectual and emotional outcomes. Positive results are supported by making students feel competent (that their actions are successful or have resulted in benefits), relatedness (connected to one another), and autonomous (giving the student a chance to be an agent) which broadly align with Macmurray's system. An implication to be drawn from Macmurray is that educational practices that are misaligned with the intention and motive of a student, generate fear, or focus only on the pragmatic mode are likely ineffective and may be harmful not just to individuals but eventually to society as well through the principle of the world as one action.

Macmurray's focus on intention and motive also implies a critique of how engineering ethics is most often taught. Ethics is central to engineering's claim to be a profession [19], and it is widely accepted that engineers who are working on products that impact health and safety should be responsible for their decisions. Furthermore, if an engineering degree program seeks ABET accreditation [80] they must determine how well students have *"an ability to recognize ethical and professional responsibilities in engineering situations and make informed judgments, which must consider the impact of engineering solutions in global, economic, environmental, and societal contexts."* Engineering ethics is generally viewed and taught as deontological, or rules-based, giving guidelines on what is right to do and placing moral (right) action above the consequences of those actions. Deontological ethics derives from Kant and places responsibility on the agent for right action. As a result, many engineering programs have a course or module on ethics embedded in the curriculum which often focus on ethics case studies and covers various ethical codes so that students have some preparation for ethical decision making.

Macmurray builds from Kant, agreeing on the importance of individual responsibility but Macmurray's emphasis on action shifts attention to being able to do what is right rather than knowing what is right to do. For an agent to do what is right requires both their intention and motive align with the moral good of supporting freedom, community, and friendship. While there will always be uncertainties in action, doing what is right stems from habit which is developed through the cycle of withdrawal and return. Thus how students practice the cycle of withdrawal and return and which modes of apperception they develop determines whether they develop habits that enable them to do what is right in the moment of action. From the continual and iterative nature of the cycle of withdrawal and return it follows that such developmental opportunities need to be embedded throughout a curriculum rather than added on as separate modules or courses [16]. This aligns with developmental learning theories such as those from Perry [110] or King and Kitchener [111]. Macmurray's focus on the person and the need to develop habitual modes of apperception that intrinsically value others is highly relevant for a discipline like engineering education that consciously or not empowers individuals to act as change agents in the world. As Norm Augustine points out, the actions of engineers have consequences [112]. Developing such habits in students is important since the ethical responsibilities of engineers can be poorly defined, geographically variable, and constrained by economics and their workplace [113]. Furthermore, the fact that engineering projects are uncertain, economically motivated and involve many stakeholders ("the problem of many hands") makes it difficult to draw clear lines of responsibility. This perspective will be explored further in discussion of the systemic mode of apperception.

Given the predominantly pragmatic focus of engineering education, ethics is often considered one of a broad set of "professional skills" that also include communication and teamwork that are necessary to engineering but are often distinguished from "technical skills" [114]. Considering the development of technical and professional skills separately may make the design of classes and curriculum and measurement of learning outcomes simpler, but from the perspective of Macmurray's system it is questionable the extent to which such skills can actually be separated. Inherent to such implicit separation is the assumption that technical and professional skills represent separate domains of knowledge and should be developed differently. Since for Macmurray knowledge is developed by action and used in action to achieve a goal then if the agent's goal is to increase their technical proficiency, then they need to use technical knowledge to develop the habits that support such proficiency. This is much of the goal of engineering education as currently practiced and the activities needed to develop such expertise have received much attention. By analogy if the agent's goal is to be professional then they should similarly use professional knowledge to develop professional habits. This analogy, however, does not suggest a clear path for curriculum development unless professional skills are further broken down into communication, teamwork, etc. as is often done. From a more holistic perspective it is difficult to accept that someone who is trained to communicate well, work on teams, knows ethics, and so forth automatically qualifies to be a professional unless these skills are integrated in action. Being professional is more than knowing, it is more related to being, or what Barnett and Coate [5] have termed making an ontological commitment and Varela identifies as spontaneity in action [115]. Rather than discrete skills a professional integrates skills and knowledge—both technical and professional—with a commitment to continue learning and developing [116]. Macmurray would likely argue that such integration or "wholeness" cannot be taught except holistically and furthermore cannot occur only through developing the pragmatic mode but rather requires other modes of apperception.

Take, for example, teamwork which has received increased focus in engineering education since the release of the EC-2000 criteria by ABET [117]. Teamwork is most often developed by having students work together in teams, often scaffolded by teaching stages of team development [118], [119] or providing peer feedback [120]. While such approaches are helpful, Macmurray's system highlights that individuals who have developed fear-based habits may withdraw from a team or seek to exert dominance. Addressing these issues, which are individual and personal, would suggest adopting a more reflective approach based on shifting ingrained habits, teaching students to recognize underlying motives, and building skills in the personal mode of apperception.

Given that personal growth occurs through the iterative cycle of withdrawal and return, it is an open question the extent to which the personal mode of apperception is developed through the homework and examination cycles that predominate in many engineering degree programs. If a degree program overemphasizes the pragmatic mode then students must learn to develop other modes independently. Such an approach risks disadvantaging the professional development of those students who, for example, do not join study groups, participate in organizations, or do other activities which may develop the personal, contemplative, and systemic modes of apperception (compare Chambliss and Takacs [121]).

Beyond the technical – professional tension, another area of debate within many engineering departments are long running discussions about the balance between theory and practice or "knowing how" vs. "knowing that"[8]. This theoretical – practical tension expresses itself in interesting ways, such as the order of courses in a curriculum or debates about the relative importance of hard vs. soft or technical vs. professional skills. From Macmurray's perspective this debate is not just "academic" since such curricular decisions impact graduates' beliefs [122] and through the principle of the world as one action help determine how the world will come to be. The dominance of Descartes' *cogito ergo sum* and the tension Kant tried to resolve between theoretical and practical reason has interesting resonances in engineering curricula such as almost universal adoption of math and science prerequisites for engineering courses. The dualism Macmurray seeks to address— that the real world is theoretical and exists independent of my perception but as an engineer I can change the world for the better—is a central tension in engineering education. Debates that stem from this dualism flare up occasionally, often when curriculum change is being considered, and can be divisive for engineering departments and hurt personal relationships. Such arguments make little sense under Macmurray's system since knowing and acting are a unity with theory arising from practice so that any attempt to divide engineering along lines of theory versus practice is misplaced. Since knowledge is secondary to action, Macmurray's framework suggests that closely connecting theory to practice is important, keeping in mind the importance of attention and the need to support multiple modes of apperception discussed earlier and shown at the top of Figure 7.1. Grounding knowledge in action makes learning relevant, which has a positive impact on students [66, pp. 83-84]. Macmurray might argue that focusing on students' emotional development in order to enable them to focus on significant questions is also critical in engineering education [40]:

> "...the rationality of our conclusions does not depend alone upon the correctness of our thinking. It depends even more upon the propriety of the questions with which we concern ourselves. The primary and critical task is the discovery of the problem. If we ask the wrong question the logical correctness of our answer is of little consequence. There is of necessity an interplay, in all human activities, between theory and practice."

Viewing engineering education through ae pragmatic lens shows most programs overemphasize this mode of apperception which in turn has led to the development of a performance-based culture which values competence and in which knowledge and skills are valued for their utility. This particularly expresses itself in curricular discussions on professional or transferrable skills, which often emphasize the utility of a person for an engineering job rather than their development as a person as an end in itself. While such transferable skills are the traits that make engineers valued in organizations, this focus comes with the opportunity cost that students do not fully develop the other three modes of apperception that Macmurray argues are necessary for human and moral development.

The Contemplative Mode of Apperception – Achieving Satisfaction

While the pragmatic mode of apperception is characterized as scientific or rational, the contemplative or artistic mode is concerned with an individual's emotional development and ability to find significance in their actions. While emotions are often considered subjective, Macmurray's system gives emotions an objective basis and hypothesizes that an individual's emotions can be developed through action in the cycle of withdrawal and return in the same way intellect is developed. In fact, by putting thought subsidiary to action, Macmurray frames emotion as the motive force for action and our actions are aimed towards what we care about [42, p. 146]:

> "What we feel and how we feel is far more important than what we think and how we think. Feeling is the stuff of which our consciousness is made, the atmosphere in which all our thinking and all our conduct is bathed. All the motives which govern and drive our lives are emotional. Love and hate, anger and fear, curiosity and joy are the springs of all that is most noble and most detestable in the history of men and nations. Scientific thought may give us power over the forces of nature, but it is feeling that determines whether we shall use that power for the increase of human happiness or for forging weapons of destruction to tear human happiness in pieces. Thought may construct the machinery of civilization, but it is feeling that drives the machine; and the more powerful the machine is, the more dangerous it is if the feelings which drive it are at fault. Feeling is more important than thought."

Under Macmurray's system determining the ends towards which engineering education works depends on the emotional valuations that underlie educational programs, policy initiatives, and accreditation systems. The question of what *should* be valued is ultimately a question for the agent, not for an organization or society, although the agent's environment affects such valuations through the theory of the world as one action.

The four modes of apperception represent different ways of perceiving the Other (the world). While the pragmatic mode is developed through rational generalization of experience, the contemplative mode is developed through contemplation which Macmurray defines as systemic, purposeful, critical, and prolonged concentration on a unique object [67, pp. 114-116] rather than a general class of objects. Macmurray viewed such contemplation as the process an artist went through as they came to understand the subject of their art[9]. Contemplation in art is done to gain a holistic and dynamic understanding, a perspective that aligns with Eisner's views on what art contributes to education [124]. The analogy in engineering education is getting to know the work of an engineer or an engineered artifact and through that the conceptual connections that underlie technology. Just as different artists choose different subjects for their work, in the case of engineering education the object of contemplation depends on what has meaning for the student. The fact that agents have different interests and backgrounds implies that the contemplative mode of apperception is individual and idiosyncratic.

Macmurray views developing the contemplative mode of apperception as a process through which an agent uses their emotions to appreciate what has value in and of itself. While all development occurs in the cycle of withdrawal and return (top of Figure 7.1), Macmurray frames several actions that develop the contemplative mode of apperception. One is to use contemplation to know an object, or in the case of engineering education some engineering work, through which an agent finds emotional valuation in the object itself. Such enjoyment of the object for its own qualities is separate from enjoyment of an internal emotional state that the object may trigger. For example, one can appreciate an amusement park ride or mobile computing device for their technological sophistication or for the entertainment they bring. Thus to develop the contemplative mode of apperception it is necessary for the agent to learn to distance herself and her ego from the object being perceived. Such emotional objectivity is defined as the ability to appreciate what is worthwhile for itself rather than more ephemeral feelings that are invoked. The opposite of emotional objectivity is sentimentality which is the deification of feeling or the belief that what we feel is what we should have. For Macmurray a society that supports sentimentality has already proceeded down a path that veers toward authoritarianism since whoever influences what we think we should have has a disproportionate effect on society. From an engineering perspective it is interesting to consider how public-private infrastructures such as information technologies run under models which rely on advertising-based revenues designed to influence human wants and the careful cultivation of social media "influencers".

The contemplative mode of apperception is also developed when the agent exercises constructive imagination by selecting, modifying, and organizing attributes of the object within their own mind to try to get to the essence of the object through a process of emotional rather than intellectual reflection. This process of internalizing and developing a unique understanding is described in Rom Harre's Vygotsky cycle shown in the bottom right of Figure 7.1, although Harre intended intellectual rather than emotional development. Much work on conceptual understanding in education aligns with this view [123]. Macmurray also highlighted that developing the contemplative mode requires that the agent develop sensibilities, or an ability to be present in and perceive the world through multiple senses or whole-body awareness. Such an ability to sense with more than the eyes and mind is necessary to freedom of action [36, p. 122]:

"If we do this, we shall find ourselves able to act in the world with the whole of our bodies, and our actions will be spontaneous, emotional, non-mechanical and free. Intellectually controlled action, in fact, is only possible through the process of inhibition. The intellect itself cannot be a source of action. All motives of action are necessarily emotional, but the intellect can use the emotion of fear to paralyse the positive emotions, leaving only that one free to determine action which corresponds to the planned purpose."

At first glance such talk of appreciation, constructive imagination, and whole-body awareness may seem foreign to the pragmatic perspective of engineering or science. However even within these disciplines such sensing occurs and often distinguishes experts from novices. An example in my own life was when as a graduate student I could walk into the research lab and tell by the sound of the pumps when something was wrong; an ability that astounded new students. This was not something that was taught, but was developed over time by building, rebuilding, and improving an experimental apparatus through a process that engaged me both intellectually and emotionally. From this description it may be that elements of the contemplative mode align with Polyani's notion of tacit knowledge [125]. There are also alignments with recent conceptions of "T-shaped" engineers [126] who have both breadth and depth; presumably the depth is developed not only by a particular but arbitrary course of study but contemplation of particular issues within the broad practice of engineering that have emotional significance to a student.

Macmurray acknowledged that it is much more difficult to develop the contemplative mode than the pragmatic mode, and gave as a reason that the contemplative mode is not as amenable to discursive explanations [36, p. 117-118]:

> "The capacity to appraise an object in this way has to be learned and it grows with exercise. To describe the process of contemplation is extremely difficult - perhaps, in the end, impossible. This is because it is not an intellectual process; it has its own mode of expression which is by means of imagery, by the construction of images. We might say that it is largely 'unconscious'; that it is not discursive but intuitive; that in the end if our reflection is successful we just know that we are right, but we cannot tell how we know and can certainly not prove that we are right."

In engineering education the word "images" should be expanded by including schema [60] and heuristics [27] in the passage above. Also relevant are the ways engineers express ideas through graphical representations. While such difficulty of description presents problems for pragmatic and process-oriented models of education, it is important to remember that the contemplative mode of apperception does not extend the agent's capacity for action as the pragmatic mode does, but rather helps to better understand one's own values and identify what will bring them satisfaction and significance. Macmurray frames the contemplative mode as identifying what is good rather than what is true, which aligns loosely with Amartya Sen's capability approach to human development and social justice [127], particularly his distinction between capabilities and functionings.

The contemplative mode of apperception determines worth, significance, and value to an agent so critiquing engineering education from this perspective must originate in the views of the agent. Here we arrive at a conceptual difficulty; since agents are unique persons any critique must be specific, idiosyncratic, and agent-centered. In other words, I cannot speak for what you should value or, if we value the same things, what aspects are of value to you. Nor does sharing the experiences of having been an engineering student and being an engineering educator allow me to speak for you because to make assumptions of value based on common roles would be to generalize not particularize. However framing the contemplative mode as determining whether the results of an action bring satisfaction allows an unconventional path forward. By drawing particular instances from my own personal experience and reflecting on them through the dual lenses of satisfaction and understanding the value of these experiences for themselves rather than the feelings they invoke, one of many possible critiques of engineering education can be framed. While this particular critique may not match your experience, it is hoped the attempt will have value in your own reflection and contemplation. This requires using autoethnography [128] and thus for a short while this chapter shifts into a first-person writing style.

My experience of being an electrical engineering faculty member stretches over more than thirty years and covers a time in which there has been significant contraction in the number of students graduating in my discipline [12]. In this context, drawn from teaching at both predominately undergraduate and land grant universities, there are many instances that stand out in my memory and many more that have likely been forgotten. Although memory is notoriously inconsistent, under Macmurray's system I am not trying to create a factual record of the past but rather reflect on how my personal satisfaction or lack thereof with past actions influenced the cycle of withdrawal and return which developed the person I am now. In this case I expect the precision of memory is less important than trying to understand my own emotional state as I reflect on the past; as discussed in previous chapters we remember what is significant to us. There are many episodes and experiences that stand out, some of which I am ashamed about and others of which I am proud, reflecting Macmurray's love – fear duality. Some of these experiences are very powerful, but I feel I must reject them because they are sentimental rather than emotionally objective. The sentimental events that induce positive emotions include hearing from parents what a difference I made in their son's or daughter's life, that a class I taught helped a student land a new job, and so forth. Similarly, my negative emotions come from critical comments in student or performance evaluations, when a student left the program because I either said the wrong thing or failed to say the right thing, or the remembered shame when I found it more convenient to stay silent than stand up for an ideal. While powerful, these events are sentimental because they evoke emotions rather than indicate intrinsic value or are related to the personal mode of apperception rather than the contemplative mode.

To write this section I took a day to reflect as honestly as possible on my career in engineering education and found there are several experiences, objects, or events that I value intrinsically for themselves rather than for the emotions they invoke. I characterize this, perhaps overly simplistically, as the difference between liking something and loving it. One may like something transiently, but love stems from the deep attachment that allows perseverance through inevitable difficulties. One of experiences I value for itself is the many times that I have taught capstone design in engineering. I experience a capstone design course as a work in progress or action research project [129] that requires small, iterative changes every time the course is taught. It is highly satisfying to see how opportunities for students' growth and development improve as a result of these iterative changes. I use the term "student growth and development" somewhat glibly because despite developing rubrics and exams or constituting expert review panels I find it difficult to precisely define let alone measure what I mean by "growth"; yet I know the improvement is real when seen through the arch of experience. I have also found lasting satisfaction when in designing a new course a concept I thought I understood comes into new focus. This might be described as the "a-ha!" moment or revelation of finally understanding something only partially understood before. A moment that stands out is when the Fourier transform finally made intuitive sense to me. Such understanding need not arise from the specific and detailed since there are similar rewards to breadth of perception of the complex and distributed. During my time serving at the National Science Foundation, I found great satisfaction in seeing how the dynamic, ceaseless, and well-intentioned activities undertaken by researchers across the country to improve engineering education intersected and built on each other. These activities were neither centrally coordinated nor completely random; rather they emerged from the collision and mixing of ideas that together helped shape the future. There was a beauty in the dance of ideas that has almost an organic character, a complex ecosystem in which the activities in defined niches somehow created conditions under which new ideas could thrive. At some level each of these examples as a unique kind of beauty.

For Macmurray these emotional valuations both arise from action and determine our future actions. What then are my own set of values, what in engineering education is beautiful to me and helps me select one action above many possible others? From a rational actor perspective teaching capstone design does not make sense since it is very stressful and requires time and dedication beyond other classes I could choose to teach. What about this experience in particular steers my actions? One factor is the immersiveness of the course, both for myself and students. There is a "realness" and "rawness" about confronting technical, personal, and organizational difficulties and overcoming them while immersed in a project that differentiates this experience from a more content-driven course. I find I like this challenge. Another factor is the fact that the time and energy I dedicate to a process of slow, iterative change leads to improvement over time. Rather than a research project, capstone design is more of a craft. Craft is a word that dates back to Old English (cræft) which historian Arthur Langlands [130] claims has become untranslatable but was originally used as an amalgamation of the knowledge, resourcefulness, and wisdom with an underlying spiritual element that comes from doing. Capstone design as cræft describes my experience well since it goes beyond the transmission of content that would take priority in other courses. I might sum this up as when I teach capstone, I get to be authentic and exist in the moment as well as develop more meaningful relationships and friendships with students.

Additionally teaching capstone has clarified other values in my own teaching. A particular experience stands out from one of the first capstone classes I taught when I didn't really know what I was doing. The project was for student teams to design a laser tag game and I allowed teams to have considerable freedom in how they implemented their designs and presented the results. The results were so creative and the end-of-semester demonstration so fun and irreverent that I can still pull up vivid images in my mind's eye over a decade later. From this I discovered I greatly value student autonomy; as I have sought to support it in my teaching and scholarship autonomy has become one of my foundational values.

The satisfaction of gaining new understanding, either of a concept or system, is harder to describe. I might label this satisfaction as truth, but that too slippery of a concept. Rather the value to me is more similar to that of a familiar landmark. While we live in an age of navigational ease where smart devices tell us exactly where to turn to get to our destination, similar technologies do not yet exist for the larger journey of life. We have lost the art of dead reckoning that was once known to navigators of the Pacific islands who "steered by the shape of the sky" in canoes designed for dynamic instability so the navigator must always pay attention to their task [131]. In my own uncertain navigation through a career in engineering education the concepts and ideas I feel I really understand and value for themselves serve as navigational landmarks that serve, in a Ptolemaic rather than Copernican view of life, as "...a light in dark places when all other lights go out." [77, ch. 8]. Koen might say such deep knowledges are my go-to heuristics [27].

As I step away from the first-person perspective, I have gained a new sense of the value a sustained reflection to separate real from sentimental emotions has had. I suspect that while your own values are likely different than mine the process I described has analogies in your own personal and professional development. Such exploration and personal reflection into satisfaction and value found in engineering education provides insights into the importance of contemplative mode of reflection. Underlying all of my personal examples is the idea of iteration, of working over a period of time to refine and improve; what one truly values improves with age. Macmurray would likely argue this is simply the meaning of cycle of withdrawal and return; to avoid pursuing sentimental fantasies and rather place emotional valuation on things outside of ourselves so we can grow over time into being fully human. In interrogating my own emotional state, I have found a sense of freedom in recognizing what I value as a person and being able to separate these activities from the actions I feel I should do; i.e., duties or obligations.

One critique of engineering education that arises from the contemplative mode of apperception is that the crowded nature of most engineering curricula and hectic pace of academic life do not leave time or offer necessary support for students or faculty to develop their own values. While no one can speak for all engineering degree programs there are few[10] that place the same value on developing the contemplative mode of apperception as they do on the pragmatic, at least at the undergraduate level. While there is an increasing interest in reflection [133], as Ellen Rose points out reflection is often used in a pragmatic mode, to improve academic performance, rather than in a contemplative mode to identify lasting values as described by Macmurray [134]. Many programs also lack sufficient curricular freedom or unstructured time for students to choose to pursue areas they find personally significant.

This critique is neither original nor new. Engineering educators and policy makers have responded to the perception that STEM disciplines are too narrow and prescriptive by exploring how to integrate arts and/or humanities into the STEM disciplines leading to STEAM or SHTEAM. A recent high-level study conducted by the United States National Academy of Sciences [63] found considerable anecdotal but little hard empirical evidence to support such integration while acknowledging the existence of cultural challenges and structural barriers. Never-the-less the report recommended more exploration and more integration between technical and human disciplines. The report, however, adopted an instrumental and pragmatic lens, focusing mainly on integration of disciplines within existing course, curriculum, and co-curricular structures and how integration supported widely desired learning outcomes. Macmurray would likely argue that because this approach fails to address the fact that the underlying reason for art and the humanities is to develop the contemplative mode of apperception attempts to integrate art into STEM which derive from a pragmatic perspective will likely be ineffective; Eisner makes similar points [124]. Instrumental approaches also fail to acknowledge the importance that beauty plays in development of societies that engineers will disproportionately contribute to. For Macmurray beauty served as a compass that pointed society towards good [42, pp. 217-218]:

> "Just as thought is concerned, in a peculiar sense, with truth, so feeling is peculiarly concerned with beauty. A morality that

looks upon feeling as something naturally dangerous and untrustworthy is a morality that despises beauty and looks upon it as a side issue. I am inclined to think that the worst feature of modern life is its failure to believe in beauty…The strongest condemnation of modern industrial life is not that it is cruel and materialistic and wearisome and false, but simply that it is ugly and has no sense of beauty."

Given the centrality of reflection and contemplation to human development, engineering students who do not develop other modes of apperception may be fated to see the world pragmatically which can limit their ability to choose meaningful ends and contribute to moral good.

Macmurray's cycle of withdrawal and return and the role the contemplative mode of apperception plays in human development offers another vision for the role of art in STEM disciplines; as a way to develop the emotional objectivity required to select meaningful problems. A degree program that emphasized developing the contemplative mode of reflection would assist students in judging whether their education is helping them to articulate and achieve personally satisfactory goals. Unlike "satisficing" in engineering design that is aimed at meeting specifications within externally imposed constraints, satisfaction involves finding personal meaning by developing the capability to reflect on whether an agent's actions satisfy their intentions. Remember that for Macmurray intention includes both the mundane—wanting to get a good grade—but also the transcendent such as gaining the capabilities that will enable the agent to change the future. The rationale for adding arts to STEM is not for students to gain creativity but to develop the ability to meaningfully contemplate the larger purpose and personal significance of education in light of their evolving values.

If a role of education is for students to clarify their beliefs and identify meaningful vocations or causes to which they can fully commit, even if temporarily, then developing the capability for students to identify what they value is necessary. Such commitment is important for learning [5], highlighting that the contemplative mode not only complements the other modes of apperception, but is critical to develop if an engineering student is to be able to use their engineering knowledge in a way they find meaningful in the future. Macmurray is clear that significance, or faith, is central to engineering contributing to good [42, p. 36]:

> "What we do with knowledge science creates is not the business of science. Science has nothing to do with good or evil, with the the satisfaction of human desires. It has nothing to do with action; because it must be completely disinterested, and action cannot be disinterested. Action depends on what we want, on our choice of what is most worth doing...Science...can only provide the means for achieving what we want to achieve. If what we want is evil or stupid or selfish, science will prove disastrous. If our wants are wise and high minded, it will be a boon...And if we begin to feel that nothing is really worth doing, we shall not use science at all or use it only to amuse ourselves and to distract our minds from the deadly boredom of living a life that has lost its meaning because we have lost our faith."

The word engineering can be substituted for science in the above passage since the demand for engineering graduates stems in part from their ability to advance military, commercial, government, and business purposes [135].

In summary, Macmurray saw the emotional objectivity developed through the contemplative mode of apperception as critical to education if it is to serve as an activity that contributes to becoming human. As always Macmurray spoke plainly and directly about forms of education which overvalued intellectual and undervalued emotional development [28]:

> "Education which emphasises rationalisation and calculation—as ours does—and neglects contemplation, has the effect of suppressing imagination and with it the natural

creativeness of its pupils. The only 'advantage' of this is that it tends to produce adults who are dull enough to enjoy routine, easy to organise for co-operation and ready to do as they are told. But from a properly educational point of view there is nothing to be said for this: it is again an educational perversity. To learn to be human is to learn to be creative."

The fact that emotional valuation derives from the person poses a challenge for engineering education since most programs have highly structured curricula. A challenge is how to provide students sufficient autonomy to choose areas of significance. It is likely that all engineering educators know of talented students who eventually chose not to pursue an engineering degree because they were not given an opportunity to align their conceptions of what was valuable in life to their degree program. Reflection on what is valuable in education matters to students; many works on retention in engineering programs speak of slowly building doubts and emotional crises before a student leaves the university [136], [137].

The Personal Mode of Apperception – Friends and Colleagues

While the pragmatic mode of apperception focuses on improving action and the contemplative mode on choosing worthwhile acts, the personal mode of apperception enables the agent to act in heterocentric manner, for others, and thus build community. Because the personal mode is outward looking it addresses morality, or the proper form of our relations with others. Macmurray's system defines the good through supporting the freedom of other persons. In brief since we can only become fully ourselves through our relations with others moral actions are those that support the freedom needed for our own and others' development as persons. When the intentions of the other agents we interact with are aligned in mutual support of each other a community is formed. For Macmurray such community is central to our development as persons because each of us relies on the good will of others for our own development; *"My freedom depends on how you behave"* [42, p. 119]. Whether the act of an agent is moral or not depends upon the agent's intention to maintain relations with others that support freedom and community, and the personal mode of apperception equips the agent to act in this way.

As with the other modes of apperception the development of the personal mode occurs through the cycle of withdrawal and return so that the agent's intention is affected by motive and attention as shown at the top of Figure 7.1. Macmurray's system thus implies that the ability of a student to act morally is determined by the extent to which the environment, activities, and relationships in a university develop the personal mode of apperception. Since modes which are reinforced become habitual and those less often utilized take conscious intention, graduates who do not sufficiently develop the personal mode of apperception may not develop the intention to be outwardly focused and less able to perceive the needs of others. Furthermore, since the actions of all agents contribute to the tone of society through the world as one action, students who do not develop the personal mode may undervalue individual freedom and contribute unwittingly to a society that trends towards authoritarianism.

These concerns are particularly relevant for engineering programs since as Macmurray points out not only are we reliant on others for becoming who we are but *"…our freedom, as individuals, depends upon the co-operation of others. We are fed and clothed by our fellows. The whole apparatus of our life is provided by others."* [41, p. 164]. These "fellows" are often engineers who play a role in the large, complex, and distributed systems—transportation, energy, communication, water, etc.—needed for maintaining human life and standards of living. The late Charles Vest framed such systems as a frontier of engineering [138] since understanding, maintaining, and scaling such systems becomes ever more critical as the Earth's human population continues to expand and her natural systems come under increasing stress. Our very freedom and survival depend on the capabilities which engineered systems have provided, and the extent of this dependency grows the more technological a society becomes. If engineers working at the intersection of engineering and public welfare are to act morally and be skillful at relating to others as persons, then they must develop the personal mode of apperception. Since Macmurray's system focuses on action, moral action in engineering education is to help students learn to do what is right rather than simply learning to know what is right to do.

Because we develop in relationship with others the personal mode of apperception is central to human growth and moral development, preparing an agent to better perceive the needs of others, develop meaningful friendships, and intentionally support community. While these arguments provide valid reasons to consider better supporting development of the personal mode in engineering education, there are also arguments against such consideration. One such argument can be made from the perspective of curriculum since the benefits of developing this mode need to be weighed against the opportunity costs. Given the amount of information engineers are asked to learn, developing the personal mode of apperception may be better addressed outside the engineering curriculum or students may enter college with this mode already sufficiently developed. Another argument from the perspective of engineering practice is that Macmurray's notions of friendship and community are altruistic, but overly utopian. It is not clear if the *a priori* assumptions about what constitutes moral good in Macmurray's system will benefit graduates who will need to function in a world predominantly driven by economic utilitarianism and neoliberal capitalism which posit different notions of good. Arguing from the perspective of inclusion, Macmurray's ideal of community may prioritize sameness over diversity and result in programs which are less equitable and serve to maintain privilege. These concerns are discussed below.

There is considerable evidence to reject the argument that it is not the role of a degree program to address issues of personal relationships, that these are better addressed outside the curriculum.

In-depth case studies [121], [139] find that friendships matter in college and have both social and academic impacts. In terms of academics, the impact can be positive or negative; the type of friendship network students have and what groups they associate with matter. The relationships students have—with peers, faculty, and staff—affect their motivation to learn. It is not the number of relationships or the structure of a student's friendships that are of primary impact [139], rather it is the quality and meaningfulness, or heterocentricity, of relationships that matters most. It is well established that offering support to others influences motivation which is central to learning [140]. Because memberships in some groups help students while belonging to others can hinder their social and academic development, the nature and form of community matters. It is the personal mode of apperception that dictates the form of our relationships—whether they are love or fear based—and this has powerful resonances for learning. There is also substantial evidence that building relationships should happen early during a student's time at the university; the advice existing students overwhelmingly have for new students is to become involved [139]. Community is central to college and some authors [121] assert that these experiences ultimately matter more to student development than pedagogy, curriculum, and facilities.

In terms of the argument that the personal mode of apperception is not relevant for engineering practice, the question seems to come down to which belief systems or mindsets an engineering education should instill in students to best prepare them for life after the university. This is an important but difficult question given that the pathways of engineering students are many and varied [15] and due to broad demand for the skills engineering programs provide are becoming more so [6]. Never-the-less as discussed previously, engineers have a disproportionate impact on society through the technologies they develop. While engineering education has always sought to better equip students to contribute to technological advances [141], as the complexity and societal embeddedness of engineering work has grown there is increasing consensus that engineers need to know more than how to design technology and act professionally [58]. One response has been to mandate learning outcomes focused on the larger context of engineering. In the United States accredited engineering degree programs must determine how well their graduates can "...*design to global, cultural, social, environmental, and economic issues; recognize ethical and professional responsibilities; and make informed judgements about such issues.*" [80]. In learning to make such judgements [142], [143] students typically apply agent-centered deontological, or duty based, codes of ethics adopted by engineering societies which place several obligations on engineers. Such codes typically put serving the public welfare first with service to clients, employers, and the profession secondary. Given that deontological ethics and Macmurray's system were based on Kant, in both systems moral behavior is related to the intention of the agent [144].

In order to make, rather than just consider, informed judgements students need knowledge but also intention and motive; their perception of others matters, and this is developed through the cycle of withdrawal and return. As Macmurray points out, there is no moral consequence without action. It can be argued that in order to serve public welfare engineers need to be able to perceive human needs which in turn requires the capability to be heterocentric in relations with others. Furthermore, making ethical decisions relies on an underlying morality upon which ethics is based. Ethics, which in the case of engineering consists of standards of professional behavior that apply to engineers as a group, differs from morality, which is personal and normative. Ethics, however, is based on morality since to serve public welfare the engineer makes implicit assumptions about what is universally good for all people. While traditionally morals have been assumed to be well developed by the time a student enters college [142], in programs that increasingly draw students from geographically and culturally diverse backgrounds who are then further fragmented into affinity groups [145], it is not clear how well this assumption holds. Furthermore, morals matter since there is not universal agreement on how to achieve the good. For example, neoliberalism's focus on economic growth in free markets differs from nationalism and both ideologies have moral and ethical consequences

[72]. By emphasizing professional ethics rather than moral good engineering neatly sidesteps many such concerns. The personal mode of apperception, however, provides a definition for moral good (discussed in the previous chapters) by emphasizing freedom, friendship, and community for persons. While Macmurray's conception of the good may not align with the enacted values of engineering practice it does align with engineering education since community and friendship are central to learning. Because engineering espouses the value of being ideologically agnostic, students need to learn how to navigate different belief systems which occur through personal relationships in community. As Newman argues, one of the ideas underlying a university is to provide a forum for students to refine these belief systems among their peers and for this friendship is a prerequisite [17].

It can also be argued that the personal definition of good offered by Macmurray is necessary if engineering is to serve the public welfare. There is, at the time this book was written, an increasing recognition of the impact that technological decisions, particularly technologies of care and artificial intelligence, have on individual lives [146], [147]. Furthermore, it can be argued that friendship and community are central, rather than peripheral, to public welfare. Recent studies have found that those who are lonely or have weak social ties suffer significant negative health effects, that being socially disconnected causes more harm that air pollution or physical inactivity [148], and that over a fifth of adults in the US and the UK report being lonely most of the time [149]. Does loneliness fall within the domain of public welfare? The National Society of Professional Engineer's code of ethics states that *"Engineers in the fulfillment of their professional duties, shall: 1) Hold paramount the safety, health, and welfare of the public. 2) Perform services only in areas of their competence..."* For pervasive and amorphous social issues such as lack of connection in an age in which ubiquitous technology is augmenting or replacing face-to-face contacts it is not clear where the bounds of public welfare lie, and which fundamentally human concerns should fall outside an engineer's area of competence. Given that social fitness is malleable [150] and ideas of community are being changed by technology [93], there are strong arguments to be made that the development of Macmurray's personal mode of apperception is necessary for engineers. Again, since action is central in Macmurray's system what matters is to be able do what is right, not just know what is right to do. To serve public welfare engineers should learn to be heterocentric in relations with others. Recent studies show, however, that engineering degree programs as currently constituted not only fail to foreground public welfare, but students' concern for public welfare declines slightly over their time in college [122].

The issue of whether the notions of community proposed by Macmurray will, in practice, address or exacerbate the serious and pervasive issues of inclusion that engineering faces is difficult to address. Macmurray himself would likely answer that exclusion is fear-based and without developing the personal mode of apperception the decisions made and structures supported by administrators, faculty, staff, and students will likely continue to promote exclusion. There is some evidence that supports this perspective. Development of an engineering student's identity is a complicated process that is highly gendered and bound tightly to the activities students undertake and the environment and structures of the community they develop in [151]. The ways in which engineering students engage with their academic work and the community can either lead to acceptance or marginalization because status is conferred by being pragmatic and productive. These values arise, however, from the pragmatic mode of apperception. Given the strong role that identity, only part of which is defined by academics, plays in establishing social norms, the communities students form often reinforce hierarchies. An example is the way Greek life influences social hierarchies in college [139], [152]. Faculty perceptions of students, which are often determined by knowledge of academic achievement, also influence these hierarchies even if they mischaracterize student accomplishment.

Such case studies serve as examples of how the dominant pragmatic mode of apperception determines the norms of an engineering community. It may be possible that focusing on development of the personal mode, particularly heterocentricity in relationships and the centrality of social factors on engineering work, could alleviate these issues. However since such hierarchies are reinforced by social structures, considerable work is needed to understand how developing the personal mode would affect existing structures. For example, simply diversifying a campus and bringing in students with other perspectives does not automatically lead to a more inclusive or equitable environment [139]. Macmurray's philosophy does suggest, however, that such efforts start with persons rather than programs.

Given the arguments outlined above that the personal mode of apperception is highly relevant to engineering education, how does Macmurray's work inform how this mode is to be developed? Unfortunately Macmurray's writings do not lay out a well-defined curriculum students can follow to develop this mode. Before discussing potential ways to develop this mode it is worth mentioning what to stop doing. Just as faculty actions, policies, and the learning environment can promote community it can also hinder its development. Since the personal mode is about developing heterocentric relationships, issues such as stereotype threat [153], micro-aggressions [154], and creating an environment that leads to lack of belonging [155] can hinder its development. Policies that emphasize student competition are likely not to support the personal mode, particularly grading on a curve.

As far as positive development of this mode, in a practical sense faculty and other mentors play a key role since the personal mode is developed through relationships. The suggestions offered by Takacs and Chambliss [121] on assigning key faculty to introductory courses and helping students find mentors to whom they can connect are highly relevant. Another point brought out by Macmurray [28] is that faculty in engineering education need to recognize that all meaningful relationships are personal and we must teach who we are, not just what we know. Current trends in engineering education such as human- or user-centered design or service learning could be helpful in developing the personal mode as long as they are not too pragmatically focused. The work of Ivan Illich, who frames the effectiveness of technology as being directly related to the level of control and agency they provide users [44], may also be informative for developing the personal mode through design.

As far as ideas for developing the personal mode which fall outside the usual boundaries of engineering education, Macmurray also framed the personal mode of apperception as a religious mode. Without going into extensive detail [10, ch. 7], in Macmurray's usage religion is the social reflection of the intention of community and thus serves to bind a community together. This usage suggests that public celebration of community is important for the development of the personal mode. Macmurray also suggests that the purpose of a Supreme Being in religion is to provide a universal Other which serves as a paragon of relationships. While engineering education is likely too secular to adopt the notion of a deity or deities[11], the notion of historical figures in engineering who idealize the personal mode is worth considering. Interestingly while it is typical to integrate the accomplishments of historical figures into science and architecture education, this is much less common in engineering. Another idea is to re-examine the ABET accreditation criteria that require a year of math and science in engineering degree programs. Rather than spending a year immersed in math and science under the assumption students first need to understand natural forces in order to engineer them, students could spend their first year understanding how to relate to others and what is means to be human by taking courses in the humanities, social sciences, art, and religion; proposals for such programs have been developed [156]. In such a program engineering would not be seen as the discipline devoted to harnessing the forces of nature for the use of man but rather as the discipline that masters all modes of apperception to prepare students to imagine a more human future [157].

The Systemic Mode of Apperception –
The Engineering Education Ecosystem

The systemic mode of apperception, which does not appear in Macmurray's work, was introduced in the previous chapter to address the fact that engineering work has systemic effects which can either enhance or harm human well-being. The effects of engineering work depend on both the work itself and the context or system in which it is embedded, making it difficult or impossible to predict all outcomes. While the language has changed over time, a well-known proverb stems from the Jewish philosopher Maimonides' writings on Tzedakah or charity: *Give a man a fish, and you feed him for a day. Teach a man to fish, and you feed him for a lifetime.* The systemic mode of apperception would add to this: *But if a nation becomes over-reliant on fishing before long you have ecosystem collapse and widespread famine*[12]. The systemic mode is positive rather than negative, reflecting love for, rather than fear of, the Other just as the personal mode reflects love towards other agents (top of Figure 7.1). As discussed previously, a mode of apperception goes beyond the educational activities usually defined as reflection since it includes both intellectual and moral perception and denotes a holistic way of seeing the world. While the personal mode considers relationships with other persons, the systemic mode corresponds to the agent's relationships with non-human systems or the Other, to use Macmurray's term for the world at large. While the form of the agent's relationship with the Other differs from the relationship with another person, human-Other relationships are illustrated by someone's love of nature or aptitude with technology.

Humankind's relation with Nature has been characterized by the biologist E. O. Wilson as *"innately emotional affiliation of human beings to other living organisms"* and is hypothesized to arise by our evolution in nature [158]. Lovelock's Gaia hypothesis, which posited that all organisms on earth form a self-regulating complex system, to which there was initially strong push-back, also reflects a relational view [159]. In the Hindu, Buddhist, and particularly the Jain religions the virtue of Ahimsa, or compassionate non-violence, extends to all life and was reflected in Albert Schweitzer's philosophy [160]. Similar notions exist for human relationships with technology or the built world. For example, Pirsig's Zen and the Art of Motorcycle Maintenance [161] vividly describes the author's relationships with both humans and machines and how tensions arise from the different ways humans view and interact with technology. A systemic technological perspective is one goal of technological literacy [162]–[164], although the interpretation of technological literacy varies between groups. The notion that some individuals are more mechanically inclined while others are more socially inclined dates back at least as far as 1924 [165] and the cultural aspect of this divide was popularized by Snow's famous lecture on the two cultures [166]. Such ideas have many reflections in education today such as the notion of digital natives [167]. Across society there are many examples of relationships of groups or individuals with larger systems. Activists such as Greenpeace seek to address environmental degradation, people look for inspiration to the lives of John Muir, Rachel Carson, and Steve Jobs, and technological quasi-religions such as belief in the singularity [168] define sub-cultures of innovators.

Viewing the systemic mode as outward facing and relational suggests several ways this mode could be supported in engineering students. One pathway is activism. Although it is not currently widely practiced in engineering education [169], [170] there is considerable evidence that student involvement or activism leads to lasting and civic-oriented identity development [171]–[173]. A more common way to enable students to perceive themselves in positive relationship with the larger systems is contextualizing engineering education within these larger systems. Many capstone design projects as well as programs like EPICS [174], Engineers Without Borders [175], and the Grand Challenge Scholars program [176] take this approach. In these and similar programs students engage with large and interdisciplinary problems, often outside their campus or peer community. A more traditional way to address the systemic mode of apperception is to offer courses or modules on systems thinking [177]. It is important, however, not to conflate systems thinking, which recognizes that systems cannot be controlled, with design thinking that seeks to achieve outcomes within constraints. As with many such distinctions there is a spectrum of approaches and the differences between can be subtle, but design thinking is often aligned with the pragmatic mode of apperception as defined in Macmurray's system. Given the perennial challenge of overstuffed curricula in most engineering programs integrating systems thinking courses may be easier to desire than to accomplish. An alternative approach would be to integrate case studies into existing courses.

As the difficulty of changing engineering curricula illustrates, the constraints to changing a system arise not just from the efforts and resources available to the change agent, but the underlying structure of the system itself [31]. For this reason it is worth considering some of the factors that could limit developing the systemic mode of apperception in engineering education programs. Crowded engineering curricula were discussed above and stem in part from exponential growth over time in diverse areas such as technology-driven endogenous economic growth, the density of transistors (Moore's Law), or information storage. The overall effect has been an information explosion and in response higher education has become more specialized over time, moving from the trivium and quadrivium (the word and the number) which go back to Plato towards increasingly defining knowledge by disciplines [178], [179]. From the perspective of the systemic mode of apperception this trend towards specialization shifts the focus of education from the person to the content due to systemic considerations caused by limited recourses – time, money, and courses in a curriculum. Macmurray framed this issue as [28]:

> "Any subject, however technical, can be used as an instrument of true education by a good teacher, provided he is allowed to do so, provide he is granted conditions which are free enough and flexible enough. On the other hand the teaching of subjects tempts the organiser and the administrator to construct curricula and to elaborate methods. Organisation is

no doubt necessary up to a point in the educational field, but it is also very dangerous. It can make real education impossible in the name of efficiency."

The pressures to create more efficient curricula are being exacerbated by the fact that the costs of higher education have risen to a point where students, parents, and policy makers increasingly focus on the return on investment which drive trends towards increasing specialization. These pressures arise from rational responses to societal trends which themselves are reflections of the dominant pragmatic mode of apperception expressed through the conception of the world as one action. The challenge for engineering education, which is by nature pragmatic, is not to mistake the systemic mode of apperception for the pragmatic and make education a means to societally mandated ends rather than a way to comprehend that the intrinsic value of our relationships to the Other is an end in itself.

Given the predominance of the pragmatic mode of apperception in engineering education, the systemic mode will likely need to be supported by difficult cultural and structural changes as well as curricular interventions. The remainder of this section speculatively explores several possible approaches which support further development and implementation of the systemic mode. One approach that is gaining traction at the policy level as this book is written is known as convergence [180] that seeks to integrate expertise across disciplines. Convergence is a synthetic framework that is applied to highly interdisciplinary problems by having experts from multiple disciplines synthesize knowledge relevant to the challenge being addressed. While convergence as currently framed is pragmatic in approach, there is an implicit recognition of the value of systemic perspectives in integrating disciplinary knowledge. More importantly, policy makers recognize that creating programs that support convergence requires cultural shifts to prevent relaxation over time back to the disciplinary structures that are deeply embedded in existing organizations. The practical recommendations that emerge from policy reports, and the funding put behind such initiatives, can reduce existing barriers should engineering educators seek to develop the systemic mode of apperception.

Another aspect relevant to developing the systemic mode are the scarcity and deficit mindsets that are often deeply embedded within educational institutions and cultures. In brief, the deficit model places the blame for poor learning outcomes on internal deficiencies of students such as limited intelligence, lack of motivation, poor upbringing, or lack of a moral compass rather than on the structural inequalities of educational and social systems [181]. A scarcity mindset [182] occurs when an individual believes that a resource— e.g. money, time, companionship—is in such short supply that it overwhelms their ability to make rational decisions; the resulting obsessive focus on the resource limits their impulse control. In Macmurray's system both deficit and scarcity mindsets are negative, or fear-based, and emerge from the pragmatic mode of apperception's emphasis on the result of action serving to improve future action or the contemplative mode's withdrawal of the agent. Viewed from the pragmatic mode, individuals who fail to benefit from their past actions can be thought to exhibit personal deficiencies. Similarly, the perception that insufficient resources are available focus both faculty and students on maximizing their own access to those resources. Such actions come at the expense of building community and are countered both by the personal mode of apperception that places value on heterocentric relationships and also the systemic mode which enables the agent to perceive the variety and abundance inherent in the larger systems which sustain life on Earth. From the perspective of the world as one action scarcity and deficit mindsets in educational systems tend to be self-replicating and help determine the habitual responses of students and faculty in the cycle of withdrawal and return. Developing the systemic mode of apperception may help students and faculty transcend the structures in which they are embedded, a first step in breaking a cycle which Macmurray believed ultimately led to authoritarianism.

Other insights into the characteristics of the systemic mode arise from philosophies of interobjectivity, which holds that an individual makes sense of the world through relationships mediated by and through objects or the environment. Davis' [183] explorations of interobjective frameworks for education finds that the disciplines of ecology and complexity science, both of which are related to systems thinking, offer insights into the forms of relationships captured by the systemic mode of apperception. While ecology generally focuses on understanding and managing ecosystems, a branch known as deep ecology [184] posits all life has equal value, similar to the virtue of ahimsa discussed above. Given that much of philosophy has set humans apart from the rest of the world, ecological frameworks seek to reestablish connections and are often framed not through development of new knowledge but by rediscovering of ways of knowing that were lost as Western civilization eliminated or assimilated indigenous cultures. In such cultures the natural world had a strong spiritual dimension that was focused on the interconnection between humans and the world in which they lived. Given the reciprocity of relations with the natural world—captured by the notion of participating rather intervening—ecological frameworks often focus on power relationships between humans and nature and thus have commonalities with liberative pedagogies [185] and feminist theories [186].

In complexity science behaviors which are not intrinsic to an individual organism or unit emerge from collective interactions between individuals. These interactions allow the collective to maintain self-coherence while adapting to changing environments. Maturana [187] has expanded the definition of cognition, and thus learning, to incorporate such adaptation. Maturana goes even further than Macmurray in refuting Descartes by framing cognition as the internal and external processes by which an organism adapts to the environment. A framework known as enactivism [188] posits our existence as humans—behaviors, language, and thought—is mediated by strong coupling to the physical and social worlds. The term "strong coupling" as used in enactivism captures the essence of the systemic mode of apperception. From this perspective the goal of the systemic mode is to understand the nature of this coupling, to learn to sense it not intellectually but through whole body sensation—

the term Macmurray used was sensuality or sense experience [28] — as a way to reflect on our actions in the cycle of withdrawal and return. Given that complex systems are distributed and have the characteristic of autopoiesis there are moral and ethical dimensions to enactivism [189]–[191] which re-examine notions of autonomy and socially distributed responsibility. Given Macmurray's focus on dynamic development through action and continual learning, complexity theories are likely a fruitful path to explore in thinking of how to develop the systemic mode of apperception in students.

The broad frameworks of ecology and complexity each provide insights for developing the systemic mode of apperception within engineering education as well as the role of engineering education in the larger systems in which it is embedded. The notion of participation that arises in ecological discourses as well as acknowledgement of the spiritual aspects of relatedness capture the outward facing aspect of the systemic mode. The concept of connectedness runs counter to the interventionist language used in founding documents for engineering, *"...the art of directing the great sources of power in Nature for the use and convenience of man..."*, and engineering education, *"...the modern conception of the professional engineer...as the creator of machines and the interpreter of their human significance, well qualified to increase the material rewards of human labor and to organize industry for the more intelligent development of men."* [14]. To develop ways of reflecting that situate engineering students as participants within a system it may be helpful to look to notions of mindfulness, which are currently receiving greater attention in education broadly [192]. Modes of apperception, however, are not just reflective activities but inform the intention and attention of an agent. Developing the view that ethical behavior is highly situated, emergent, and involves knowing-doing-being simultaneously [115] fits both with Macmurray's focus on development and habituation, but also suggests a moral imperative to develop an expertise of self.

From complexity science a conclusion is that learning, which is very broadly defined, arises not only internally within the agent but from the structure of the environment and the types of connectivity it enables. From this perspective at least part of a student's development is an emergent phenomenon that can be helped or hindered by their environment. The systemic mode implies that it is as important to focus on structures within educational systems as on pedagogies and content. From the viewpoint of complexity, it is not just the individual student that is important, but the collective of students and faculty that are structurally coupled together in the learning environment. In thinking of a collective it is helpful to remember that traditional students aren't necessarily seeking to become successful engineers but rather successful students, and it thus falls to faculty and staff to align being a student with becoming an engineer. As Macmurray highlights, education is social and emotional as well as intellectual and if students are to become successful engineers their environment has to support such holistic development. Environments which enable emergence, at least for simple entities, are those that are balanced. One balance is between similarity and diversity since agents who are too dissimilar cannot communicate effectively while those that are identical do not provide the differences needed for emergence. Another balance is between structure and freedom where students are guided towards meaningful objectives but the manner in which they achieve them is left open so novelty can emerge.

The idea of connectivity also provides a lens to look at engineering education more broadly. While there are certain advantages to defining engineering education as a discipline, from the systemic perspective such efforts should also look at the connecting role played by engineering education in the larger ecosystem that includes government, industry, foundations, accreditors, and many others. Given the breadth of engineering education and the fact that students from engineering are sought across many fields, it may be more germane to view engineering education, like optics and photonics [193], as an enabling discipline which provides value to others, but which does not have a well-defined disciplinary home. The value of engineering education in this model is achieved not only by the specialized knowledges and terminology it creates, but its ability to connect diverse niches in the larger ecosystem. An ecological analogy is that of a keystone species, one that is highly networked to other species and has a large effect on the ecological community in which it exists.

Viewing the dynamic and heterogeneous practices of engineering education critically from the perspective of ecology and complexity two additional areas seem fruitful in developing the systemic mode of apperception: student autonomy and narrative.   Student autonomy or agency broadly addresses both a goal of education — after college graduates will need to continue to learn without access to formal instruction — and the actions that bring this goal about [194]. Some level of autonomy is important because the Other is effectively incomprehensible in its whole and so our relationship with it is determined through the lens of our own actions. Given the myriad possible foci of the systemic mode of apperception, it seems unrealistic to rely on curriculum to fully determine the type or form of these relationships. It may be better to consider the development of the systemic mode as requiring both structured knowledge, e.g., systems thinking, as well as giving students the freedom to develop a personal affinity with some aspects of the Other through the work they do in their degree program. Because of the experiential nature of such development and the fact that this relationship is spiritual, emotional, and intellectual more than rational perception is required. The psychologist Jerome Bruner [195], echoed later by Kahneman [73], posited that we have both rational (logico-scientific) and narrative ways of processing information and sense-making occurs through stories as much as reason. The narrative mode aligns with Macmurray's system since this form of understanding strives for situatedness and connection to others and our process of constructing stories about alternative realities is an ongoing, recursive process that leads to generalized abstractions about the Other. In other words, we build the systemic mode of apperception both by understanding systems and relating to them in a personal and narrative way. The role of stories in this mode are that they enable agents, systems, events, reasons, and resources to be placed in a meaningful temporal sequence – a plot. Developing narratives places the student in a position not only to understand the complex Other but to see themselves in relation to it both in the past and the future [196]. There has been relatively little work using narrative in engineering education [197], [198].

Not surprisingly many of the narratives within engineering education are technological [78]. Given that engineering has essentially contributed to creating a built world that is increasingly replacing the natural world, technology is an integral part of the Other for engineers and thus determines aspects of the systemic mode of apperception. Facer [93], has explored how Macmurray's philosophy is relevant to an increasingly socio-technical world in which notions of community and friendship are being changed by information technologies. She finds that technology can either support or undermine such relationships with the future as yet uncertain as to the overall effects. For engineering this is a key question since engineers are the designers of many technologies which have been found to depersonalize relationships [146], [147], [199] and result in social inequities. However all technology changes human relationships [200], and technologies can open up new forms of relationships as well as change existing ones. The seductive potential of technology is to extend the notion of community beyond geographic boundaries, and in a real sense this has been accomplished. Yet unlike natural systems, technological systems are built in the larger context of human needs and wants. Macmurray's philosophy thus provides a way to understand the effect of intentions and motive on the form and effect of human-built systems. One rationale for developing the systemic mode of apperception within engineering education is to enable engineers to step away from the pragmatic, means-centered focus to look more reflectively at the systemic impact of their work. From the perspective of creating future developers of technology the centrality of reciprocity and relationships to Macmurray's conception of moral good as focusing on enhancing the freedom of others may help guide development of the systemic mode.

Summary

In summary, this chapter has critiqued engineering education from the perspective of the pragmatic, contemplative, personal, and systemic modes of apperception.   The strongest critique of engineering education is the degree to which it is adopts the pragmatic mode leading to an over-emphasis on education as a means and corresponding neglect of the ends it serves. By placing too much focus on intellectual pursuits that create generalizable knowledge engineering risks becoming so focused on efficiency that it loses its regard for persons.   In other words, if engineering educators train engineers to only reflect on their actions from a pragmatic mode of apperception they are contributing to creating organizations and societies that undervalue being human, the consequences of which are profound. During Macmurray's life he saw the rise of modes of thinking that undervalued human freedom and led to the rise of communism and fascism [34]. Although one might claim such concerns are outdated today, the issues Macmurray raises about authoritarianism are increasingly being discussed about the consequences of neoliberal capitalism [69] and unfettered adoption of technology. Through the lens of "the world as one action" if engineers are trained to see the world only pragmatically then over time the profession becomes a means to an end and potentially isolated from the world we inhabit. The relative invisibility of engineering in society is well documented [201].

Integral to Macmurray's work is the notion that all modes of apperception form a unity which contribute to the holistic development of a person.   While pragmatism is central to the contingent, heuristic-driven practice of engineering, Macmurray, like Newman [17], vigorously argues that education is not about being trained for a role, but about becoming human [28]:

"Universities are educational institutions, as are schools. Their business is not primarily to produce scientists, or historians, or philosophers, but through the science and humanities, through discussion in their societies or through games in their athletic club, to educate men and women. And education, from the standpoint of its victims, is learning to be human."

One can argue that specialized training for engineering students is necessary if they are to fulfill the societal functions required by the engineering profession, but this argument in essence limits freedom for both students and society by thinking of engineering education, and thus students, as a means to an end. If alignment with existing societal needs is required to support education or if a degree program does not support developing self-agency even at personal risk, neither freedom nor agency is supported. If education is about becoming human, then it is a mistake to conflate the value of education to an individual with its societal value. Predictably engineering education has adopted the pragmatic perspective of engineering and often falls into the error of claiming societal value through efficiency, by trying to produce and qualify many copies of the same product. Macmurray's view of education as part of the process of becoming human highlights that the value of education to society is not by educating all students to meet some external standard, but rather through the aggregate of all educated individuals, their knowledge, and their connections to each other. We are inextricably part of the system in which we exist.

8
CONVERGENCE AND SYNTHESIS

"Personal reality is a matter of degree. We are not endowed with
reality at birth; we have to create our own reality by continuous
effort and struggle. We are all more or less unreal. Our business is
to make ourselves a little more real than we are."

Macmurray, *Freedom in the Modern World*, p. 210

As the last chapter sought to critique engineering education divergently through the lens of the four modes of apperception, this chapter concludes the exploration of the questions asked in the preface and introduction by synthesizing the main points and seeking to converge to a conclusion. The term conclusion is somewhat disingenuous since philosophy never provides answers, rather it serves to get people to ask better questions and, like Newman's view of a university course [17], develops:

"...a clear, conscious view of their own opinions and judgements, a truth in developing them, an eloquence in expressing them, and a force in urging them...to see things as they are, to go right to the point, to disentangle a skein of thought to detect what is sophistical and to discard what is irrelevant."

The preface and introduction raised two questions: in what ways does engineering education claim to serve moral good, and how does engineering education justify its existence as a worthwhile end in itself rather than merely as means to others' ends? These questions were explored using the philosophical system of John Macmurray. This system arose out of the social crises that followed the First World War and questioned existing political and economic systems that Macmurray saw as undermining human freedom. The first five chapters summarized elements of his personal and critical system and a sixth chapter added to his system. These ideas were then expanded upon in chapter seven to focus more specifically on engineering education which is claimed has a large and underappreciated impact on society. During the exploration of these questions, and others raised along the journey, several themes repeated themselves in different contexts and explorations. This chapter summarizes these interwoven themes which are intended to serve as points of departure rather than a destination.

The theme that resonates perhaps most strongly in Macmurray's work is the importance of learning to become fully human, a process that is as difficult as it is vital. Four ideals underlie what it means to be human: having sufficient freedom to be able to develop into who we really are, the willingness to test our beliefs against reality so we can act in a way that is meaningful, an underlying faith that frees and guides our emotions so we can find significance in life, and adopting the moral stance that recognizes we develop through others and our own freedom depends on supporting theirs. These ideals cannot be achieved by an agent in isolation, rather they can only be developed through others and in community. Education plays a role in this development, but not the only role since all an agent's actions are encompassed by the cycle of withdrawal and return which we as persons go through continuously. Whether education helps or hinders the process of becoming human depends on the extent to which it supports friendship and community and acts from a motive of love rather than fear. There are various beliefs about what the purpose of education should be—continuation of a discipline, supporting economic needs, etc. [57]—but for Macmurray all of these are secondary to, and build from, the foundation of becoming a person. Becoming human is the underlying purpose of education. Macmurray's philosophy thus suggests a reprioritization for engineering education. Curricular constraints and growth of knowledge pressures engineering educators to adopt a scarcity mindset; there is a competition for time within a curriculum, and never enough time to accomplish what we think is needed. Macmurray's work suggests that while all the aims of education are important, there will never be enough time, and the goal of the engineering educator is to create an environment for growth rather than design the perfect curriculum. Such efforts require reassessing and balancing competing priorities. From this perspective what matters in education is supporting the cycle of withdrawal and return for each student in a way that develops all four modes of apperception. The value of education—engineering or otherwise—is the extent to which it encourages friendship and community and enables students to better support the development of other persons [202] in whatever path they take through life.

Also foundational to Macmurray's philosophy is that we become human not through thought but through action, from which thought is resultant and secondary. Action drives the cycle of withdrawal and return and what we learn through our actions determines who we become. The implications for engineering education are obvious and well-recognized if not always widely implemented; active learning works [203]. Yet action by itself is not sufficient for learning [204], it has to be tied to directed attention, meaningful reflection, and supported by opportunities to iteratively act again based on what is learned. A heuristic is simply to recognize that over time we become what we intend to do. Becoming requires commitment and commitment requires emotional valuation, which in turn requires education develop emotions as well as the intellect. As discussed elsewhere an under-developed mode of curriculum is the aspect of becoming [5], [205].

One of the major themes that emerged from looking at engineering education through the lens of Macmurray's system is a recognition of the extent to which the values of engineering have been adopted into educational practices. In particular the education of engineers overemphasizes the pragmatic mode of apperception at the expense of the contemplative, personal, and systemic modes. Engineering education's focus on a pragmatic view of the world provides an education that is substantively incomplete. To put it more bluntly, engineering degree programs mostly choose to educate engineers at the expense of educating persons. It is worth remembering that an engineering education is the only college education most students will receive, and the more engineering education monopolizes students' time the less room there is for other types of learning. Macmurray's system implies that the characteristics of engineers who graduate from various degree programs depend upon the modes of apperception developed in college. Given research showing the development of the brain extends into the mid-twenties [206], and the fact that college is many students' first encounter with engineering, the experiences they have in college are likely foundational to their development as engineers. While students may learn the contemplative and personal modes through their electives, extra-curricular activities, and friendships these are usually considered peripheral to the engineering curriculum. Since the pragmatic mode focuses on means, engineering education as currently practiced does not help students learn the emotional valuation needed to determine what ends are significant to them, echoing Mitcham's criticism of engineering [16]. As research in engineering education has increasingly embraced the social sciences, it is similarly time for the practice of engineering education to broaden its perspective and begin to explore how to better develop all four modes of apperception. If engineering education continues to limit its attentions to preparing students who focus only on pragmatic questions ultimately engineers will contribute to a society so focused on efficiency that it has no place for being human.

There is another aspect to engineering education's over-emphasis on means: by learning to perceive the world pragmatically the agent generalizes their experience to produce ever more effective ways of accomplishing their goal of advancing the state of the art [27]. While such innovation plays a vital role in the economy, it means engineers are always working to eliminate or undermine their current function; to stay relevant engineers must evolve their own function at least as fast as they evolve the technology that automates that function. Keeping up becomes more difficult as the technological rate of change accelerates[13]. Another, more positive, way to look at this issue is that technology continually emancipates engineering, making it easier to learn and do. One need only look to the Maker movement [207] to see how those without a formal engineering education do for fun the functions engineers performed in the not-so-distant past. From the perspective of systems thinking the fact that technology, the product of engineering, is coupled to the function of engineering creates a reinforcing, or positive feedback, loop. This scenario raises a challenge for engineering education which is tasked with preparing graduates for engineering careers under the constraints of time and money, particularly in disciplines where technology is advancing quickly. Macmurray has no answers to this dilemma except to point out that perhaps the role of engineering education is not to prepare engineers but rather to play a role in the development of humans who over time may become engineers.

Although engineering education tends to focus on the pragmatic mode of apperception, a theme that runs throughout Macmurray's work is the importance of developing all modes to develop holistically as a person. To briefly summarize, the pragmatic mode lets the agent improve their ability to act, to become more effective. The contemplative mode focuses on developing emotional objectivity so the agent can choose problems that have significance. The personal mode of apperception, which is arguably the most important, develops the moral capacity to perceive the needs of others and build heterocentric relationships that support their freedom. The systemic mode focuses on developing positive relationships with the larger systems in which the agent is embedded and see how their actions affect these systems. In other words: develop the intellect, develop the emotions, develop the ability to relate well with others since they determine your future, and develop the ability to place yourself and your actions in the context of the world. From this perspective Macmurray's system outlines one possible reconception of a U.S. liberal arts education that is not focused on areas of study, but rather the basic ways a person needs to perceive the world to develop their full humanity.

While a balanced development of the four modes of apperception certainly sounds inspirational, it is not clear how well it plays out in practice given the reality that the increasing cost of college puts increasing pressure on students to develop skills that pay off in the short run. Such concerns are particularly true for those students who must strain their economic resources to attend college. This is an important criticism, and one higher education is struggling with as it seeks to balance competing missions and the needs of an expanding number of disciplines. Modes of apperception, however, are not disciplines since they do not provide an a priori structure from which to build understanding. Rather the four modes of apperception provide a framework that administrators and faculty can use, like Bloom's Taxonomy [208], to frame and analyze the types of learning experiences that take place across a curriculum. Again, the theme of learning to be human resonates strongly here; is a curriculum more than development within a discipline and if so, what provides overarching coherence to the myriad of experiences that make up college? The answer, as with most such questions in higher education, depends on the student. It is important then for a university to focus on commonalities rather than differences in student experiences; certainly, becoming human is a good starting point for the difficult discussions higher education is facing.

Another theme that cuts across this critique was the cyclical rhythm of withdrawal and return which is shown in Figures 3.1 and 6.1, and at the top of Figure 7.1. Macmurray's system highlights the dynamic and continuous nature of this action – knowledge cycle through which we are constantly developing as humans throughout our lives. The temptation in engineering education is to think of education through a disciplinary lens – as a set of knowledge, skills, and experiences that in sum produce an engineer. As discussed before this reflects the pragmatic nature of engineering work but loses sight of the fact that all experiences are interpreted by students who are continuously going through the cycle of withdrawal and return. Or as a colleague once said: *"The students are always learning, just not always what we are teaching."* The cycle of withdrawal and return points out that who we become is determined by what we intend (intention), the emotional context that modifies intention (motive), what results we choose to focus on when we act (attention), and how we reflect on the results of our actions (modes of apperception). Given the developmental nature of college—both its *raison d'être* and the plasticity of the adolescent brain—the fact that over time the cycle of withdrawal and return becomes habitual places a large moral obligation on educators. The habits that students learn in college stick with them for life. Such embeddedness highlights that engineering education exists within, and with outcomes inseparable from, the larger university. Learning environments, social interactions, and academic and administrative structures all contribute to who students eventually become [121].

While popular criticisms of college often point out that students don't learn much during their time in college [209] perhaps learning—at least that which can be measured by even psychometrically valid exams—is actually a secondary effect of college. Macmurray's system emphasizes that learning also consists of developing habits that either contribute to becoming human or inhibit this development. Key to becoming fully human is the empowering effect of love and inhibitory effect of fear. The policy dialogs around engineering education often have a strong note of fear: if we don't fix [insert concern of the moment] then the results will be catastrophic for our society. This dialog often cuts across scales of the larger ecosystem, from faculty all the way to those policy makers who inhabit the halls of power and finds its way down to students through the curricula, courses, and interventions that stem from perceptions motivated by fear. Things need not be this way. Macmurray's work gives cause for hope as a quote at the top of chapter six illustrates: *"Fear not; the things that you are afraid of are quite likely going to happen to you, but they are nothing to be afraid of."* What college teaches is habits, the ability to act well in the moment, and this may be enough if done well. Students continue to grow and learn after they leave college. As Varela's enactivist essays on ethical know-how point out, the best actions and highest virtues arise from assiduously practicing the habits that allow a person to act both wisely and spontaneously in the moment [115]. The systems-based definitions of cognition proposed by Varela [187] imply that learning may not be causal, an assumption that underlies almost all work in engineering education. Despite the many calls for higher education to develop creativity, critical thinking, professional and other instrumental skills these may in fact distract from, rather than focus, the mission of higher education. The world of tomorrow will not be that of today, education is always handicapped by an inability to predict the future. However, by carefully crafting the environments and experiences through which students develop the habits that let them become both engineers and humans we may prepare people who can act wisely and justly and who find the world of tomorrow different but not frightening.

The theme of embeddedness or scale-invariance, i.e., similarities across scales, also runs through this exploration of engineering education. Through Macmurray's principle of the world as one action the acts of an individual are both affected by and affect society. The habits we develop throughout our lives and within a degree program are broadly reflected in society at large and will act to shape that society in the future. As discussed in chapter five, we have a choice of whether or not to believe that our actions shape the future, and if we do, we must choose whether or not we live in a way that enacts this belief. This seems very abstract and philosophical, but for engineering educators who are tasked with supporting student development the implications are significant. At one level the implication of the world as one action combined with the continuous nature of the cycle and withdrawal and return means our actions matter. The learning environments we create, the mentoring we do, the small selfless acts on behalf of students are refracted and reflected in ways we can never know. So are our rejections, lack of compassion, and the stories we tell about how students have changed since we ourselves were students; fear multiplies differences. At another level it is not just our actions that matter but the way our own habitual modes of apperception are enacted on a day-to-day basis. If our perceptions are grounded in fear, if our day-to-day actions do not reflect the world we want to be, if we do not intend freedom for others then it is this world we unconsciously recreate. At this level engineering education is not just about student development, it is also about how our own growth as persons affects the future. A key heuristic in systems thinking is that you should first determine your own role in the problem you are trying to solve [91].

The world as one action also suggests we begin to view engineering education as an ecosystem in which all entities both contribute to and draw from the larger environment which is both constrained and dynamic. Although individuals may occupy a particular niche, they are connected by various degrees of coupling to others across the larger ecosystem. Like an ecosystem engineering education is resilient if it is diverse enough to enable emergence, connected enough to enable resources to flow, and wise enough to find the optimal level of organization (keystone species) needed to maintain coherence. However, unlike natural ecologies humans are agents whose actions can be intentional and who shift between niches throughout their lives. As the cost of higher education rises, new forms of credentials are beginning to emerge, and as the nature of work changes students are increasing finding a variety of pathways through educational ecosystems [210]. Such mobility, the increasing freedom students have, presents new challenges for the students navigating these ecosystems and the educators responsible for evolving and maintaining them.

Navigation is a useful analogy in such scenarios. In the last chapter rational Western views of navigation based on maps and instruments was differentiated from navigation in indigenous cultures which is contingent, immediate, and based in experience [131]. Key to indigenous or Ptolemaic forms of navigation, which are arguably more descriptive of student experience that the curricular charts faculty produce, is the role heuristics play in making moment-to-moment decisions. One of the themes in Macmurray's work that can serve as a navigational heuristic is emotional valuation, which he terms significance. While educators often look at education through a rational lens—what is the correct order of topics to develop needed expertise—the emotional lens of significance likely plays a larger role in student decisions. Years ago, I was giving a talk about engineering education to a group of students and one student asked of all the problems in engineering education, which was the single most pressing? After some thought I answered that somehow we had made learning not fun anymore. In reflecting on that encounter I think I got the answer only partially right. While failing to have fun is a symptom of the deeper issues, if I had to answer again I would say that engineering education lacks the significance it could have. How significant, how meaningful, are the experiences we craft for students and who is it that ultimately determines that significance, the teacher or the learner? The challenge arises in balancing disciplinary requirements with supporting sufficient student autonomy to make learning have meaning. While we use many theories to explain meaning and motivation—e.g., logotherapy [211], self-determination theory [106], or social cognitive career theory [212]—at the end of the day we all want to feel as if we are living. For Macmurray significance is closely related to freedom [42, p. 114]:

> "...all activities which are really significant for us are spontaneous. It is the feeling of constraint and bondage in our activities that makes them seem unsatisfactory to us. The sense of freedom is our guarantee that we are making the best of life. When it is lacking we are thwarted and forced to live in a way that does not express our sense of the meaning of life."

In conclusion, how do the themes that cut across this exploration of engineering education through the lens of Macmurray's philosophy inform the two questions posed earlier: how does engineering education claim to serve moral good, and what are the ends of an engineering education? Macmurray makes clear throughout his work that moral good is defined through enabling persons to have the freedom to develop into themselves. This freedom has different aspects: freedom from material constraints; the freedom to grow, develop, and adapt to our community; and the freedom to be spontaneous and make true friends. An engineering education serves good to the extent it develops and supports these freedoms and evil if it serves to inhibit them.

We become human through continually enacting the rhythm of withdrawal and return as we act and reflect in a constellation of other actors. We are not isolated thinkers except when we reflect, and we need these others to become ourselves. We become who we are through action, and our learning is enabled by being ourselves rather than hiding ourselves in fear of what others may think. We are constantly learning—supported to become who we are meant to be by love and inhibited by fear—by developing habits which let us react in the moment. If we are fortunate enough to have a well-rounded education (that is, we practice all modes of apperception) we gain wisdom and the ability to act well in the moment not from due rational consideration but from habituated awareness. If instead we are limited in our perceptions, our path in life is likely more limited. As engineers and educators we are responsible for actions and decisions that affect others, and for this education is necessary but not sufficient. To be able to contribute to good we must choose to live as if our actions continually remake the world rather than are independent of it. We must ground ourselves in reality and develop the emotional objectivity needed to have faith our actions in the world will be significant. None of this is easy, and becomes almost impossible if we are inhibited by fear or fail to develop meaningful friendships either through our own cowardice or because we are not supported by the environments and systems that surround us.

Macmurray's philosophy emphasizes that engineering education, like all education, is to help us continuously learn to become human which we can only do through others. This is the answer to the second question: the end of engineering education is to become human, and the ends are indistinguishable from the means. We must become human by trying to be human. The principle of the world as one action highlights that we are asked to choose whether our life is for ourselves or part of something greater. If we choose the latter path we have an obligation to steer our own development towards promoting freedoms which enable others to become persons. This answers the first question: we serve moral good by ourselves becoming human and supporting that development in others. It should not come as a surprise that there really weren't two questions, simply the same question phrased different ways. It may well be that all the questions we ask in engineering education are just facets of the same question framed through our own interests and experience: how do we become fully human?

NOTES

"Nothing that is not inherently beautiful is really good"

Macmurray, *Freedom in the Modern World*, p. 149

1] Unfortunately, this makes Macmurray's work more difficult to find and cite.

2] An example of such constraint from the Renaissance is Galileo Galilei's forced recantation of his claim the earth moved around the sun due to its conflict with religious orthodoxy which took all worthwhile knowledge as already known from scripture. Here the intellectual life was constrained or not free.

3] An alternative treatment of two ways of perceiving the world through either logico-scientific (rational) or narrative thinking processes is developed by Jerome Bruner in *Actual Minds, Possible Worlds* [195].

4] An example of events serving as the cause of external emotions is a firebrand politician who calls forth feelings from voters who both revel in the emotion and turn inwardly, hoarding their righteous indignation and savoring the feelings that were invoked. These feelings are unreal because they inwards-focused and not connected to a real person against which they can be tested and refined. If a voter had a friendship with that politician so they were connected personally then real emotion is involved.

5] Macmurray also describes the personal mode of apperception as religious since the development of fellowship has generally been considered a function of religion. Macmurray frames religion as necessary for rational growth while rejecting Freud's view of religion as regression, Marx's view of religion as an opiate of the masses [213], and religion's more supernatural aspects. Macmurray distinguishes real from fraudulent religions through how they represent fear. To Macmurray fake religions promise imaginary wish fulfillment:

"Shut your eyes to things you are afraid of; pretend that everything is for the best in the best of all possible worlds; and there are ways and means of getting the diving powers on your side, so that you will be protected from the things you are afraid of. They may happen to other people, but God will see to it that they don't happen to you."

Real religions on the other hand help people deal with fear by saying:

"Look the facts you are afraid of in the face; see them in all their brutality and ugliness; and you will find, not that they are unreal, but that they are not to be feared." [41, p. 63].

Thus, for Macmurray religion is not escapism or a way to abrogate responsibility, both of which increase fear, but rather it serves as a means to emphasize intention towards community and strengthen the community's will towards fellowship in order to make relationships love- rather than fear-based.

6] In *Persons in Relations* Macmurray uses the term "State" when talking about societies dominated by negative modes of apperception since fascism and communism were the issues of his time. Today authoritarian states are on the rise, but new issues of justice are beginning to emerge around corporate capitalism and neoliberal economic policies. Sedlacek in *The Economics of Good and Evil* explores many of these issues [72]. For example, US law opened the door to grant personhood to corporations in 1868 when the 14th amendment to the Constitution was passed. In recent decades, particularly since the Citizens United v. Federal Election Commission decision in the US Supreme court, corporations are increasingly gaining rights once reserved to humans.

7] *"The totality is not, as it were, a mere heap, but the whole is something besides the parts."* Metaphysics, Book VIII, 1045a.8–10

8] Such discussions stem from ancient Greek philosophers who distinguished between *episteme and techne.*

9] Such concentration can be illustrated by the parable about a Chinese emperor who was overly fond of his elderly cat. He commissioned the greatest painter in the empire to immortalize the cat and the painter agreed subject to the proviso he could take the cat back to his studio until the picture was complete; although he had some misgivings the emperor agreed. As months went by and neither cat nor painting appeared and the emperor's dispatches went unanswered or were curtly answered "still working", the emperor became increasingly nervous until, followed by his retinue, he rode out to visit the painter. On entering the studio, the emperor saw it was filled with paintings of his cat, each more wonderful than the last. The emperor flew into a rage and demanded to have the best painting and his cat right now, to which the artist replied he was not yet done. The emperor would not bend so the painter stepped up to a blank canvas and in a few brushstrokes created a painting that so captured the nature of the emperor's cat the monarch was brought to tears at the beauty of the work. When the emperor asked why in the name of Heaven the artist hadn't just created the painting at the palace the artist pointed at the many earlier paintings and replied that without months of contemplative practice it would have been impossible to create such a painting.

10] An exception to this rule known to the author is the Iron Range Engineering program.

11] The author must admit a personal fondness for this idea, perhaps similar to the *Lares* and *Penates* of Roman times.

12] Note that while memorable this proverb is not strictly true. The work of economist Elinor Ostrum has shown communities that have maintained and benefited from ecological systems she calls common pool resources that have lasted for millennia [214]. Key to longevity and sustainability are systematic rules and practices implemented by all members of a community, which align well with many elements of Macmurray's philosophy.

13] An interesting compendium of curves illustrating progress in technology can be found at the performance curve dataset hosted by the Santa Fe Institute [215].

BIBLIOGRAPHY

[1] J. R. R. Tolkien, *The Lord of the Rings, Part III The Return of the King*. New York: Ballantine Books, 1954.

[2] T. S. Kuhn, *The Structure of Scientific Revolutions*. Chicago: University of Chicago Press, 1962.

[3] R. A. Cheville and J. Heywood, "Tensions Between Industry and Academia: Policy Making and Curriculum Development," in *The Engineering-Business Nexus: Symbiosis, Tension, and Co-Evolution*, S. H. Christensen, B. Delahousse, C. Didier, M. Meganck, and M. Murphey, Eds. Cham, Switzerland: Springer, 2019, pp. 475–498.

[4] P. Taylor et al., "Is College Worth It? College Presidents, Public Assess Value, Quality and Mission of Higher Education," Pew Research Center, Washington, DC, 2011.

[5] R. Barnett and K. Coate, *Engaging the Curriculum in Higher Education*. London: Open University Press, 2004.

[6] A. P. Carnevale, N. Smith, and M. Melton, "STEM," Center on Education and the Workforce, Georgetown University, Washington, DC, 2011.

[7] College Board, "Trends in College Pricing," *Education*, p. 44, 2015.

[8] T. Piketty and E. Saez, "Inequality in the long run," *Science*, vol. 344, no. 6186, pp. 838–843, 2014.

[9] P. Korkki, "The Ripple Effects of Rising Student Debt," *New York Times*, 24 May 2014.

[10]   P. Senge, The Fifth Discipline: *The Art & Practice of The Learning Organization*. New York: Doubleday, 2006.

[11]   F. McCluskey and M. L. Winter, *The Idea of the Digital University*. Washginton, DC: Westphalia Press, 2012.

[12]   National Science Board, "Science and Engineering Indicators 2012," National Science Foundation, Arlington VA, 2012.

[13]   J. Altonji and S. Zimmerman, "The Costs of and Net Returns to College Major," Cambridge, MA, 2017.

[14]   C. R. Mann and M. Press, "A Study of Engineering Education," Carnegie Foundation for the Advancement of Teaching, Boston, 1918.

[15]   Committee on Understanding the Engineering Education-Workforce Continuum, "Understanding the Educational and Career Pathways of Engineers," Washington, DC, 2018.

[16]   C. Mitcham, "The True Grand Challenge for Engineering: Self-Knowledge," *Issues in Science and Technology*, vol. 31, no. 1, 2014.

[17]   J. H. Newman, *The Idea of a University Defined and Illustrated: In Nine Discourses Delivered to the Catholics of Dublin*. Project Gutenberg, 1852.

[18]   T. D. Williams and J. O. Bengtsson, "Personalism," *The Stanford Encyclopedia of Philosophy*, 2018. [Online]. Available: https://plato.stanford.edu/archives/win2018/entries/personalism/.

[19]   B. J. Kallenberg, *By Design: Ethics, Theology, and the Practice of Engineering*. Eugene, Oregon: Cascade Books, 2013.

[20]   G. Lichtenstein, H. L. Chen, K. A. Smith, and T. A. Maldonado, "Retention and persistence of women and minorities along the engineering pathway in the United States," in *Cambridge Handbook of Engineering Education Research*, New York: Cambridge University Press, 2015, pp. 311–334.

[21]   D. M. Riley, A. Slaton, and A. L. Pawley, "Social Justice and Inclusion," in *Cambridge Handbook of Engineering Education*, A. Jorhi and B. M. Olds, Eds. New York: Cambridge University Press, 2014, pp. 335–356.

[22]   S. M. Lord, R. A. Layton, and M. W. Ohland, "Trajectories of Electrical Engineering and Computer Engineering Students by Race and Gender," *IEEE Trans. Educ*, vol. 54, pp. 610–618, 2011.

[23]   S. L. Goldman, "Why we need a philosophy of engineering: a work in progress," *Interdiscip. Sci. Rev.*, vol. 29, pp. 163–176, 2004.

[24]   E. Conlon, "Prisoners of the Capitalist Machine: Captivity and the Coroporate Engineer," in *The Engineering-Business Nexus: Symbiosis, Tension, and Co-Evolution*, Cham, Switzerland: Springer, 2019, pp. 39–60.

[25]   W. R. Bowen, *Engineering Ethics: Outline of an Aspirational Approach*. London: Springer-Verlag, 2009.

[26]   S. L. Goldman, "The Social Captivity of Engineering," in *Critical Perspectives on Nonacademic Science and Engineering*, P. Durbin, Ed. Bethlehem, PA: Lehigh University Press, 1991.

[27]   B. V. Koen, *Discussion of the Method: Conducting the Engineer's Approach to Problem Solving*. Oxford: Oxford University Press, 2003.

[28]   J. Macmurray, "Learning to be Human, with introduction by Michael Fielding," *Oxford Rev. Educ.*, vol. 38, no. 6, pp. 661–675, 2012.

[29]   D. Snowden and M. Boone, "Leader's Framework for Decision Making - Harvard Business Review," *Harv. Bus. Rev.*, 2007.

[30]   H. W. J. Rittel and M. M. Webber, "Dilemmas in a general theory of planning," *Policy Sci.*, vol. 4, no. 2, pp. 155–169, 1973.

[31]   D. H. Meadows, *Thinking in Systems: A Primer*. White River, Vermont: Chelsea Green Publishing, 2008.

[32]   D. H. Meadows, "Dancing With Systems," *Syst. Thinker*, vol. 13, no. 2, 2002.

[33]   The John Templeton Foundation, "The Gifford Lectures," 2016. [Online]. Available: http://www.giffordlectures.org/.

[34]   J. E. Costello, *John MacMurray, A Biography*. Edinburgh: Floris Books, 2002.

[35]   F. G. Kirkpatrick, *Macmurray: Community Beyond Political Philosophy*. Oxford: Rowman & Littlefield, 2005.

[36]   P. Conford, *The Personal World: John Macmurray on Self and Society*. Edinburgh: Floris Books, 1997.

[37]   P. Hunt, "A public philosopher, John MacMurray and the BBC, 1930 to 1941," 2001. [Online]. Available: http://johnmacmurray.org/wp-content/uploads/2011/03/JM-and-the-BBC-Philip-Hunt.pdf.

[38]   M. Fielding (Ed.), "Learning to be Human: the educational legacy of John Macmurray," *Oxford Rev. Educ.*, vol. 38, no. 6, pp. 653–781, 2002.

[39]   "The John MacMurray Fellowship Website," 2014. [Online]. Available: http://johnmacmurray.org/.

[40]   J. MacMurray, *The Self as Agent*. London: Faber & Faber, 1957.

[41]   J. MacMurray, *Persons in Relation*. London: Faber & Faber, 1961.

[42]   J. Macmurray, *Freedom in the Modern World*, 2nd ed. London: Faber & Faber, 1932.

[43]   P. Friere, *Pedagogy of the Oppressed (30th anniversary edition)*. New York: Bloomsbury, 2000.

[44]   I. Illich, *Tools for Conviviality*. London: Marion Boyar, 2001.

[45]   S. Frezza and D. Nordquest, "Engineering Insight. The Philosophy of Bernard Lonergan applied to Engineering Knowledge Generation," in *Philosophy and Engineering Education: New Perspectives Volume 2. Practical Ways of Knowing*, San Rafael, CA: Morgan & Claypool, 2019.

[46]   M. Pigliucci, *How to Be a Stoic: Using Ancient Philosophy to Live a Modern Life*. New York: Basic Books, 2017.

[47]   R. Descartes, *A Discourse On The Method*. Oxford: Oxford University Press, 2006.

[48]   G. Bassett and J. Krupczak Jr., "Abstract Thought in Engineering and Science: Theory and Design," in *Philosophy and Engineering Education: New Perspectives*, San Rafael, CA: Morgan & Claypool, 2019.

[49]   A. Schopenhauer, *The World as Will and Representation, vol. 1*. New York: Cambridge University Press, 2010.

[50]   M. Buber, *I and Thou*. Eastford, CT: Martino, 2010.

[51]   K. Davis, "Extreme Social Isolation of a Child," *Am. J. Sociol.*, vol. 45, pp. 554–565, 1940.

[52]   S. J. Suomi, M. L. Collins, H. F. Harlow, and G. C. Ruppenthal, "Effects of maternal and peer separations on young monkeys," *J. Child Psychol. Psychiatry Allied Discip.*, vol. 17, no. 1, pp. 101–112, 1976.

[53]   J. E. Froyd, P. C. Wankat, and K. A. Smith, "Five Major Shifts in 100 Years of Engineering Education," *Proc. IEEE*, vol. 100, pp. 1344–1360, 2012.

[54]   L. Menand, *The Metaphysical Club: A Story of Ideas in America*. New York: Farrar, Straus and Giroux, 2001.

[55]   R. Korte, "Implications of Pragmatism and Practice Theories for Engineering Practice," in *Philosophy and Engineering Education: New Perspectives, Vol. 2 Practical Ways of Knowing*, San Rafael, CA: Morgan & Claypool, 2019.

[56]   M. Mina, "John Dewey's Philosophical Perspectives and Engineering Education," in *Philosophy and Engineering Education: New Perspectives, Vol. 2 Practical Ways of Knowing*, San Rafael, CA: Morgan & Claypool, 2019.

[57]   M. S. Schiro, *Curriculum Theory: Conflicting Visions and Enduring Concerns*. Los Angeles: Sage, 2008.

[58]   G. W. Clough et al., *The Engineer of 2020: Visions of Engineering in the New Century*. Washington, DC: National Academcy Press, 2004.

[59]   J. Doty, *Into the Magic Shop: A Neurosurgeon's Quest to Discover the Mysteries of the Brain and Secrets of the Heart*. New York: Avery, 2017.

[60]   M. B. McVee, K. Dunsmore, and J. R. Gavelek, "Schema Theory Revisited," *Rev. Ed. Res.*, vol. 75, no. 4, pp. 531–566, 2005.

[61]   W. James, *Talks to Teachers on Psychology: And to Students on Some of Life's Ideals*. Rockville, MD: Arc Manor, 2008.

[62]   Grinter Report, "Report on evaluation of engineering education (reprint of the 1955 report)," *J. Eng. Educ.*, vol. 93, no. 1, pp. 74–94, 1994.

[63]   National Academies of Sciences, Engineering, and Medicine, "The Integration of the Humanities and Arts with Sciences, Engineering, and Medicine in Higher Education," National Academy Press, Washington D.C., 2018.

[64]   L. Bucciarelli, *Designing Engineers*. Cambridge, MA: The MIT Press , 1996.

[65]   R. A. Cheville and J. Heywood, "Drafting a Code of Ethics for Engineering Education," in *Frontiers in Education*, 2015.

[66]   P. van Inwagen and M. Sullivan, "Metaphysics," *The Stanford Encyclopedia of Philosophy*. Calfornia, 2014.

[67]   C. L. Dym, A. M. Agogino, O. Eris, D. D. Frey, and L. J. Leifer, "Engineering Design Thinking, Teaching, and Learning," *J. Eng. Educ.*, vol. 94, p. 103, 2005.

[68]   K. L. Tonso, "Engineering Identity," in *The Cambridge Handbook of Engineering Education Research*, A. Johri and B. M. Olds, Eds. New York: Canbridge University Press, 2014, pp. 267–282.

[69]   R. B. Reich, *Saving Capitalism For the Many, Not the Few*. New York: Alfred A. Knopf, 2016.

[70]   A. Giddens, *Social Theory and Modern Sociology*. Cambridge: Polity Press, 1987.

[71]   T. Hobbes, *Leviathan*. London: Penguin Classics, 1982.

[72]   T. Sedlacek, *Economics of Good and Evil: The Quest for Economic Meaning from Gilgamesh to Wall Street*. New York: Oxford, 2011.

[73]   D. Kahneman, *Thinking, Fast and Slow*. New York: Farrar, Strauss, and Giroux, 2011.

[74]   J.-J. Rousseau, *The Social Contract*. London: Penguin Classics, 1968.

[75]   Plato, *The Republic*. New York: Dover, 2000.

[76]   C. Duhigg, "What Google Learned From Its Quest to Build the Perfect Team," *New York Times Magazine*, New York Times, New York, p. 20, 2016.

[77]   C. Mitcham, *Thinking through technology: the path between engineering and philosophy*. Chicago: University of Chicago Press, 1994.

[78]   A. L. Pawley, "Universalized Narratives: Patterns in How Faculty Members Define 'Engineering,'" *J. Eng. Educ.*, vol. 98, pp. 309–319, 2009.

[79]   J. Trevelyan, *The Making of an Expert Engineer*. London: CRC Press, 2014.

[80]   Accreditation Board for Engineering and Technology, "Criteria for Accrediting Engineering Programs, 2019 – 2020," Engineering Accreditation Commision, Baltimore, 2019.

[81]   N. Cross, *Designerly Ways of Knowing*. Basel: Birkhauser, 2006.

[82]   G. Kelly, *The Psychology of Personal Constructs Volume one: A theory of personality*. London: Routledge, 1991.

[83]   L. Von Bertanlanffy, "The history and status of general systems theory," *Acad. Manag. J.*, vol. 15, no. 4, pp. 407–426, 1972.

[84]   C. J. Atman, D. Kilgore, and A. McKenna, "Characterizing Design Learning: A Mixed-Methods Study of Engineering Designers Use of Language," *J. Eng. Educ.*, vol. 97, p. 309, 2008.

[85]   J. Krupczak and G. Bassett, "Work in progress: Abstraction as a vector: Distinguishing engineering and science," in *Proceedings - Frontiers in Education Conference*, FIE, 2012.

[86]   W. Steffen et al., *Global Change and the Earth System: A Planet Under Pressure*. Berlin: Springer-Verlag, 2004.

[87]   C. West Churchman, *The Systems Approach*. New York: Dell, 1984.

[88]   Department of Defense Systems Management College, *Systems Engineering Fundamentals*. Fort Belvoir, VA: Defense Acquisition University Press, 2001.

[89]   C. Haskins, K. Forsberg, M. Krueger, D. Walden, and D. Hamelin, "Systems engineering handbook," in *INCOSE*, 2006.

[90]   L. B. Barnes, *Organizational Systems and Engineering Groups*. Cambridge, MA: Harvard University Press, 1960.

[91]   D. P. Stroh, *Systems Thinking For Social Change: A Practical Guide to Solving Complex Problems, Avoiding Unintended Consequences, and Achieving Lasting Results*. White River Junction, VT: Chelsea Green Publishing , 2015.

[92]   F. E. Ritter, G. D. Baxter, E. F. Churchill, F. E. Ritter, G. D. Baxter, and E. F. Churchill, "User-Centered Systems Design: A Brief History," in *Foundations for Designing User-Centered Systems*, London: Springer, 2014.

[93]   K. Facer, "Personal, relational, and beautifl: education, technologies and John Macmurray's philosophy," in *Learning to be Human*, London: Routledge, 2015, pp. 57–74.

[94]   J. Habermas, *Moral Consciousness and Communicative Action*. Cambridge, MA: MIT Press, 1990.

[95]   M. Kelly, *Critique and Power: Recasting the Foucault/Habermas Debate*. Cambridge, MA: MIT Press, 1994.

[96]   The Steering Committee of the National Engineering Education Research Council, "The research agenda for the new discipline of engineering education," *J. Eng. Educ.*, vol. 95, no. 4, pp. 259–262, 2006.

[97]   C. J. Finelli, M. Borrego, and G. Rasoulifar, "Development of a taxonomy of keywords for engineering education research1," *Australas. J. Eng. Educ.*, vol. 21, no. 1, pp. 1–16, 2016.

[98]   B. Seely, "'Patterns in the History of Engineering Education Reform: A Brief Essay,'" in *Educating the engineer of 2020: Adapting engineering education to the new century*, Washington D.C.: National Academcy Press, 2005, pp. 114–130.

[99]   D. A. Kolb, *Experiential Learning: Experience as The Source of Learning and Development*. Upper Saddle River, New Jersey: FT Press, 1984.

[100]   R. Harre, *Personal Being*. Cambridge, MA: Harvard University Press, 1984.

[101]   J. Cowan, *On Becoming an Innovative University Teacher. Reflection in Action*, 2nd ed. Maidenhead, UK: Open University Press, 2006.

[102]   J. Driver, "A selective review of selective attention research from the past century," *British Journal of Psychology*, vol. 92, no. 1. pp. 53–78, 2001.

[103]   H. A. Simon, "The Role of Attention in Cognition," in *The Brain, Cognition, and Education*, Orlando, FL: Academic Press, 1986, pp. 105–115.

[104]   C. J. Atman and K. M. Bursic, "Verbal Protocol Analysis as a Method to Document Engineering Student Design Processes," *J. Eng. Educ.*, vol. 87, pp. 121–132, 1998.

[105]   T. D. Wilson and P. W. Linville, "Improving the academic performance of college freshmen: Attribution therapy revisited," *J. Pers. Soc. Psychol.*, vol. 42, no. 2, p. 367, 1982.

[106]   R. M. Ryan and E. L. Deci, "Intrinsic and Extrinsic Motivations: Classic Definitions and New Directions," *Contemp. Educ. Psych.*, vol. 25, pp. 54–67, 2000.

[107]   C. Stefanou, J. D. Stolk, M. Prince, J. C. Chen, and S. M. Lord, "Self-regulation and autonomy in problem- and project-based

learning environments," *Act. Learn. High. Educ.*, vol. 14, no. 2, pp. 109–122, 2013.

[108]   L. Vanasupa, J. Stolk, and T. Harding, "Application of self-determination and self-regulation theories to course design: Planting the seeds for adaptive expertise," *Int. J. Eng. Educ.*, vol. 26, no. 4, pp. 914–929, 2010.

[109]   S. M. M. Loyens, J. Magda, and R. M. J. P. Rikers, "Self-directed learning in problem-based learning and its relationships with self-regulated learning," *Educ. Psychol. Rev.*, vol. 20, pp. 411–427, 2008.

[110]   W. G. Perry, "Cognitive and ethical growth: The making of meaning," in *The Modern American College*, A. W. Chickering, Ed. San Francisco: Jossey-Bass, 1981, pp. 76–116.

[111]   P. M. King and K. S. Kitchener, *Developing reflective judgment:understanding and promoting intellectual growth and critical thinking in adolescents and adults.* San Francisco: Jossey-Bass, 1994.

[112]   N. R. Augustine, "Ethics and the Second Law of Thermodynamics," *Bridg.*, vol. 32, no. 3, pp. 4–7, 2002.

[113]   C. Didier, "Engineering Ethics," in *A Companion to the Philosophy of Technology*, J. K. B. Olsen, S. A. Pedersen, and V. F. Hendricks, Eds. New York: John Wiley & Sons, 2009.

[114]   K. Litchfield, A. Javernick-Will, and A. Maul, "Technical and Professional Skills of Engineers Involved and Not Involved in Engineering Service," *J. Eng. Educ.*, vol. 105, no. 1, pp. 70–92, 2016.

[115]   F. J. Varela, *Ethical know-how: action, wisdom, and cognition.* Stanford, CA: Stanford University Press, 1999.

[116]   E. Hoyle, "Professionalization and deprofessionalization," in *Professional Development of Teachers: World Year Book of Education*, 1980, E. Hoyle and J. Megarry, Eds. London: Kogan Page, 1980.

[117]　J. F. Volkwein, L. R. Lattuca, P. T. Terenzini, L. C. Strauss, and J. Sukhbaatar, "Engineering Change: A Study of the Impact of EC2000," *Int. J. Eng. Educ.*, vol. 20, no. 3, pp. 318–328, 2004.

[118]　K. A. Smith, *Teamwork and Project Management*. New York: McGraw Hill, 2014.

[119]　B. W. Tuckman, "Developmental sequence in small groups," *Psychol. Bull.*, vol. 63, no. 6, pp. 384–399, 1965.

[120]　M. W. Ohland et al., "The comprehensive assessment of team member effectiveness: Development of a behaviorally anchored rating scale for self- and peer evaluation," *Acad. Manag. Learn. Educ.*, vol. 11, no. 4, pp. 609–630, 2012.

[121]　D. F. Chambliss and C. G. Takacs, *How College Works*. Cambridge, MA: Harvard University Press, 2014.

[122]　E. A. Cech, "Culture of Disengagement in Engineering Education?," *Sci. Technol. Hum. Values*, vol. 39, no. 1, pp. 42–72, 2014.

[123]　S. A. Ambrose, M. W. Bridges, M. DiPietro, and M. C. Lovett, *How Learning Works: Seven Research-Based Principles for Smart Teaching* . San Francisco: Jossey-Bass, 2010.

[124]　E. W. Eisner, *What the arts teach and how it shows*. New Haven: Yale University Press, 2002.

[125]　M. Polyani, *The Tacit Dimension*. Garden City, NY: Doubleday & Co., 1966.

[126]　D. L. Johnston, "Scientists Become Managers-The 'T'-Shaped Man," *EE Eng. Manag. Rev.*, vol. 6, no. 3, p. 67, 1978.

[127]　A. Sen, J. Muellbauer, and G. Hawthorn, *The Standard of Living*. New York: Cambridge, 1987.

[128] H. Chang, *Autoethnography as Method*. London: Routledge, 2016.

[129] G. M. Bodner and M. Orgill, *Theoretical Frameworks for Research in Chemistry/Science Education*. New York: Prentice-Hall, 2007.

[130] A. Langlands, *Craeft: An Inquiry into the Origins and Meanings of Traditional Crafts*. New York: Faber & Faber, 2017.

[131] T. Gladwin, *East is a Big Bird: Navigation and Logic on Puluwat Atoll*. Cambridge, MA: Harvard University Press, 1995.

[132] J. R. R. Tolkien, *The Lord of The Rings, Part I The Fellowship of the Ring*. New York: Ballantine Books, 1954.

[133] J. Turns, K. E. Shroyer, T. L. Lovins, and C. J. Atman, "Understanding Reflection Activities Broadly," in *Annual Conference of the American Society for Engineering Education*, 2017, p. #18388.

[134] E. Rose, *On Reflection*. Toroto: Canadian Scholars' Press, 2013.

[135] S. H. Christensen, B. Delahousse, C. Didier, M. Meganck, and M. Murphy, "General Introduction: The Business-Engineering Nexus: Nature, History, Context, Tensions," in *The Engineering-Business Nexus: Symbiosis, Tension, and Co-Evolution*, S. H. Christensen, B. Delahousse, C. Didier, M. Meganck, and M. Murphy, Eds. Cham, Switzerland: Springer Nature, 2019, pp. 1–24.

[136] M. Meyer and S. Marx, "Engineering Dropouts: A Qualitative Examination of Why Undergraduates Leave Engineering," *J. Eng. Educ.*, vol. 103, no. 4, pp. 525–548, 2014.

[137] E. Seymour and N. Hewitt, "Talking About Leaving: Factors Contributing to High Attrition Rates Among Science, Mathematics, and Engineering Undergraduate Majors," Bureau of Sociological Research, University of Colorado, Boulder, CO, 1994.

[138]   C. M. Vest, "Educating Engineers for 2020 and Beyond," 2005. [Online]. Available: http://www.engineeringchallenges.org/cms/ 7126/7639.aspx.

[139]   J. M. McCabe, *Connecting in College: How Friendship Networks Matter for Academic and Social Success*. Chicago: University Of Chicago Press, 2016.

[140]   A. W. Gouldner, "The Norm of Reciprocity: A Preliminary Statement," *Am. Sociol. Rev.*, vol. 25, no. 2, pp. 161–178, 1960.

[141]   R. A. Cheville, "Defining Engineering Education," *American Society for Engineering Education*. Indianapolis, IN, 2014.

[142]   C. E. Harris Jr., M. Davis, M. S. Pritchard, and M. J. Rabins, "Engineering Ethics: What? Why? How? And When?," *J. Eng. Educ.*, vol. 85, no. 2, pp. 93–96, 1996.

[143]   J. L. Hess and G. Fore, "A Systematic Literature Review of US Engineering Ethics Interventions," *Sci. Eng. Ethics*, vol. 24, no. 2, pp. 551–583, 2018.

[144]   L. Alexander and M. Moore, "Deontological Ethics," *The Stanford Encyclopedia of Philosophy*, 2016. [Online]. Available: https://plato.stanford.edu/archives/win2016/entries/ethics-deontological/.

[145]   J. P. Gee, *Situated Language and Learning*. New York: Routledge, 2004.

[146]   J. P. How, "Ethically Aligned Design: A Vision for Prioritizing Human Well-being with Autonomous and Intelligent Systems - Version 2," *IEEE Control Systems*, 2017. .

[147]   C. O'Neil, *Weapons of Math Destruction*. New York: Broadway Books, 2017.

[148]   J. Holt-Lunstad, T. B. Smith, and J. B. Layton, "Social relationships and mortality risk: a meta-analytic review.," *PLoS Med.*, vol. 7, no. 7, p. e1000316, 2010.

[149]   B. DiJulio, L. Hamel, C. Munana, and M. Bordie, "Loneliness and Social Isolation in the United States, the United Kingdom, and Japan: An International Survey," San Francisco, 2018.

[150]   J. T. Cacioppo and S. Cacioppo, "The Social Muscle," *Harvard Business Review*, Oct-2017.

[151]   K. Tonso, *On the outskirts of engineering: Learning identity, gender and power via engineering practice*. Rotterdam: Sense Publishers, 2007.

[152]   K. Tonso, "Teams that Work: Campus Culture, Engineer Identity, and Social Interactions," *J. Eng. Educ.*, vol. 95, p. 25, 2006.

[153]   C. M. Steele, *Whistling Vivaldi: how stereotypes affect us and what we can do*. New York: W. W. Norton & Co., 2011.

[154]   D. W. Sue, *Microaggressions in Everyday Life: Race, Gender, and Sexual Orientation*. Hoboken, N. J.: J. Wiley & Sons, 2010.

[155]   S. Headden and S. McKay, "Motivation Matters: How New Research Can Help Teachers Boost Student Engagement," Stanford, CA, 2015.

[156]   L. L. Bucciarelli and D. E. Drew, "Liberal studies in engineering – a design plan," *Eng. Stud.*, vol. 7, no. 2–3, pp. 103–122, 2015.

[157]   P. A. Vesilind, *Engineering Peace and Justice: The Responsibility of Engineers to Society*. London: Springer, 2010.

[158]   E. O. Wilson, "Biophilia and the Conservation Ethic," in The *Biophilia Hypothesis*, Washington D.C.: Island Press, 1993, pp. 31–41.

[159]   J. Lovelock, Gaia: *A New Look at Life on Earth*. Oxford: Oxford University Press, 1987.

[160]   A. Schweitzer, *The philosophy of civilization*, 1st ed. New York: Macmillan, 1949.

[161]   R. M. Pirsig, *Zen and the Art of Motorcycle Maintenance*. New York: Harper-Collins, 1974.

[162]   J. R. Dakers, "Defining Technological Literacy, Towards an Epistemological Framework." Palgrave-Macmillan, New York, 2006.

[163]   E. Garmire and G. Pearson, "Tech Tally: Approaches to Assessing Technological Literacy," National Academy of Engineering, Washington DC, 2006.

[164]   J. Blake and J. Krupczak Jr., "Distinguishing Engineering and Technological Literacy," *Philos. Perspect. Eng. Technol. Lit.*, vol. 1, pp. 3–25, 2014.

[165]   M. Freyd, "The personalities of the socially and mechanically inclined: A study of the differences in personality between men whose primary interest is social and men whose primary interest is in machines.," *Psychol. Monogr.*, vol. 33, no. 4, pp. i–101, 1924.

[166]   C. P. Snow, *The Two Cultures and the Scientific Revolution*. London: Cambridge University Press, 1959.

[167]   S. Bennett, K. Maton, and L. Kervin, "The 'digital natives' debate: A critical review of the evidence," *Br. J. Educ. Technol.*, vol. 39, no. 5, pp. 775–786, 2008.

[168]   R. Kurzweil, *The singularity is near*. London: Viking Press, 2005.

[169]   D. M. Riley, "Power. Systems. Engineering. Traveling Lines of Resistance in Academic Institutions," in *Engineering education*

for social justice: Critical explorations and opportunities, Dordrecht: Springer, 2013, pp. 41–66.

[170]   D. Riley, L. Claris, Paul-Schultz, and I. N, Ngambeki, "Learning/assessment: A tool for assessing liberative pedagogies in engineering education," in *ASEE Annual Conference and Exposition*, 2006.

[171]   K. A. Renn, "LGBT Student Leaders and Queer Activists: Identities of Lesbian, Gay, Bisexual, Transgender, and Queer Identified College Student Leaders and Activists," *J. Coll. Stud. Dev.*, vol. 48, no. 3, pp. 311–330, 2007.

[172]   B. Kirshner, "Introduction: Youth activism as a context for learning and development," *Am. Behav. Sci.*, vol. 51, no. 3, pp. 367–369, 2007.

[173]   J. Youniss, J. A. McLellan, Y. Su, and M. Yates, "The role of community service in identity development: Normative, unconventional, and deviant orientations," *J. Adolesc. Res.*, vol. 14, no. 2, pp. 248–261, 1999.

[174]   E. J. Coyle and L. H. Jamieson, "Projects that Matter: Concepts and Models for Service-Learning in Engineering," in *EPICS: Service Learning by Design - Engineering Projects in Community Service*, E. Tsang, Ed. American Assoc. for Higher Ed., 2000, pp. 59–74.

[175]   C. R. Johnston, D. J. Caswell, and G. M. Armitage, "Developing environmental awareness in engineers through Engineers Without Borders and sustainable design projects," *Int. J. Environ. Stud.*, vol. 64, no. 4, pp. 501–506, 2007.

[176]   National Academy of Engineering, "National Academy of Engineering Grand Challenge Scholars," 2012. [Online]. Available: http://www.grandchallengescholars.org/.

[177]   P. Godfrey, R. Deakin Crick, and S. Huang, "Systems Thinking, Systems Design and Learning Power in Engineering Education," *Int. J. Eng. Educ.*, vol. 30, no. 1, pp. 112–127, 2014.

[178]   M. Young and J. Muller, "Three Educational Scenarios for the Future: lessons from the sociology of knowledge," *Eur. J. Educ.*, vol. 45, no. 1, pp. 11–27, 2010.

[179]   J. Muller, "The future of knowledge and skills in science and technology higher education," *High. Educ.*, vol. 70, no. 3, pp. 409–416, 2015.

[180]   Committee on Key Challenge Areas for Convergence and Health, *Convergence: Facilitating Transdisciplinary Integration of Life Science, Physical Sciences, Engineering, and Beyond*. Washington D.C.: National Academcy Press, 2014.

[181]   R. R. Valencia, "Conceptualizing the Notion of Deficit Thinking," in *The Evolution of Deficit Thinking: Educational Thought and Practice*, London: Routledge-Falmer, 1997, pp. 1–12.

[182]   S. Mullainathan and S. Eldar, *Scarcity: why having so little means so much*. New York: Henry Holt and Co., 2013.

[183]   B. Davis, *Inventions of Teaching: A Genealogy*. New York: Routledge, 2009.

[184]   A. Naess, "The Shallow and the Deep, Long-Range Ecology Movement: A Summary," *Inq. (United Kingdom)*, vol. 16, no. 1–4, pp. 95–100, 1973.

[185]   D. M. Riley, "Employing Liberative Pedagogies in Engineering Education," *J. Women Minor. Sci. Eng.*, vol. 9, no. 2, pp. 30–32, 2003.

[186]   K. E. Ferguson, "Feminist Theory Today," *Annu. Rev. Polit. Sci.*, vol. 20, pp. 269–286, 2017.

[187]   H. R. Maturana, "Biology of Cognition," in *Autopoiesis and Cognition: The Realization of the Living*, Dordrecht: D. Reidel Publishing Company, 1980.

[188]   F. J. Varela, E. Thompson, and E. Rosch, *The Embodied Mind: Cognitive Science and Human Experience*. Cambridge, MA: MIT Press, 2016.

[189]   T. Heijmeskamp, "Ethical Know-How and the Ethical World: Towards an embodied, situated account of ethical agency," Erasmus University Rotterdam, 2017.

[190]   M. Cash, "Cognition without borders: 'Third wave' socially distributed cognition and relational autonomy," *Cogn. Syst. Res.*, vol. 25–26, pp. 61–71, 2013.

[191]   G. Colombetti and S. Torrance, "Emotion and ethics: An inter-(en)active approach," *Phenomenol. Cogn. Sci.*, vol. 8, pp. 505–526, 2009.

[192]   J. C. Felver, C. E. Celis-de Hoyos, K. Tezanos, and N. N. Singh, "A Systematic Review of Mindfulness-Based Interventions for Youth in School Settings," *Mindfulness (N. Y).*, vol. 7, pp. 34–45, 2016.

[193]   Committee on Optical Science and Engineering, *Harnessing light: Optical science and engineering in the 21st century*. Washington, D. C.: National Academy Press, 1998.

[194]   D. Boud, "Moving towards autonomy," in *Developing Student Autonomy in Learning*, D. Boud, Ed. Milton Park: Taylor & Francis, 1988.

[195]   J. Bruner, *Actual Minds, Possible Worlds*. Cambridge, MA: Harvard University Press, 1987.

[196]   H. Tsoukas and M. J. Hatch, "Complex thinking, complex practice: The case for a narrative approach to organizational complexity," *Hum. Relations*, vol. 54, no. 8, pp. 979–1013, 2001.

[197]   J. M. Case and G. Light, "Emerging methodologies in engineering education research," *J. Eng. Educ.*, vol. 100, no. 1, pp. 186–210, 2011.

[198]   G. P. Halada and P. H. Khost, "The Use of Narrative in Undergraduate Engineering Education," in *American Society for Engineering Education Annual Conference*, 2017, p. 20044.

[199]   J. Lanier, *Who Owns the Future?* New York: Simon & Schuster, 2013.

[200]   W. Powers, *Hamlet's BlackBerry: Building a Good Life in the Digital Age*. New York: Harper-Collins, 2010.

[201]   Committee on Public Understanding of Engineering Messages, *Changing the Conversation: Messages for Improving Public Understanding of Engineering*. Washington, DC: National Academies Press, 2008.

[202]   M. Fielding, "Education is if people matter: John Macmurray, community and the struggle for democracy," in *Learning to be Human: the educational legacy of John Macmurray*, London: Routledge, 2015, pp. 23–40.

[203]   S. Freeman et al., "Active learning increases student performance in science, engineering, and mathematics," *Proc. Natl. Acad. Sci.*, vol. 111, no. 23, pp. 8410–8415, 2014.

[204]   P. A. Kirschner, J. Sweller, and R. E. Clark, "Why Minimal Guidance During Instruction Does Not Work:," *Educ. Psychol.*, vol. 41, no. 2, pp. 75–86, 2006.

[205]   R. A. Cheville, "Linking capabilities to functionings: adapting narrative forms from role-playing games to education," *High. Educ.*, vol. 71, pp. 805–818, 2016.

[206]   S. J. Blakemore, *Inventing Ourselves: The Secret Life of the Teenage Brain*. London: Doubleday, 2018.

[207]   Deloitte Center for the Edge and Maker Media, "Impact of the maker movement," 2013.

[208]   L. W. Anderson and D. R. Krathwold, "A Taxonomy for Learning, Teaching, and Assessing: A Revision of Bloom's Taxonomy of Educational Objectives." Longman, New York, 2001.

[209]   R. Arum and J. Roska, *Academically Adrift: Limited Learning on College Campuses*. Chicago: University Of Chicago Press, 2011.

[210]   S. Malcolm and M. Feder, "Barriers and Opportunities for 2-Year and 4-Year STEM Degrees: Systemic Change to Support Students' Diverse Pathways." National Academies Press, Washington, DC, 2016.

[211]   V. Frankl, *Man's Search for Meaning*. Boston, MA: Beacon Press, 2006.

[212]   R. W. Lent, S. D. Brown, and G. Hackett, "Social Cognitive Career Theory," in *Career Choice and Development*, 4th ed., D. Brown, Ed. San Francisco: Jossey-Bass, 2002, p. 255.

[213]   K. Marx, *Critique of Hegel's "Philosophy Of Right."* Cambridge: Cambridge University Press, 1971.

[214]   E. Ostrum, *Governing the Commons: The Evolution of Institutions for Collective Action (Political Economy of Institutions and Decisions)*. Cambridge, MA: Cambridge University Press, 1990.

[215]   B. Nagy, J. D. Farmer, Q. M. Bui, and J. E. Trancik, "Statistical basis for predicting technological progress," *PLoS One*, vol. 8, p. e52669, 2013.